COLOR AND VICTORIAN PHOTOGRAPHY

Key Texts in Victorian Photography

Series Editor: Jennifer Green-Lewis

This series offers a collection of themed sourcebooks, curated by scholars from a variety of fields. As well as reproducing well-known texts from photography's history, each volume also introduces significant lesser-known pieces, inviting fresh discussion and new ways of thinking about photography throughout the long nineteenth century.

COLOR AND VICTORIAN PHOTOGRAPHY

Edited by
LINDSAY SMITH

Routledge
Taylor & Francis Group
LONDON AND NEW YORK

First published 2020 by Bloomsbury Academic

Published 2020 by Routledge
2 Park Square, Milton Park, Abingdon, Oxon OX14 4RN
605 Third Avenue, New York, NY 10017

Routledge is an imprint of the Taylor & Francis Group, an informa business

A catalogue record for this book is available from the British Library.

A catalog record for this book is available from the Library of Congress.

Series: Key Texts in Victorian Photography

Typeset by RefineCatch Limited, Bungay, Suffolk

ISBN 13: 978-1-4742-6421-1 (hbk)

ISBN 13: 978-1-4742-6420-4 (pbk)

CONTENTS

ILLUSTRATIONS

Plates

Figures

Introduction

"It was COLOUR that was wanting to crown all the other improvements and give perfection to the whole."

RICHARD BEARD, *FURTHER IMPROVEMENTS IN PHOTOGRAPHY*, 1843

"To what extent can we compare black and white to yellow, red and blue, and to what extent can't we?"

LUDWIG WITTGENSTEIN, *REMARKS ON COLOUR*, III, 37

Today, color is as ubiquitous as the photographic image to which it is intimately bound. Instantaneous photography available on camera phones provides unprecedented access to the reproduction of a polychromatic world. When we flick through, or electronically "send," photographs, their colors attach to them. But this seamless relationship of color to the photographic image is comparatively recent. Early photographs did not carry colors with them in this way. Yet, nor were they straightforwardly black and white. A desire to photograph was, from the first, a desire to photograph in color. The earliest inverted images produced in the dark chamber of the camera obscura were polychromatic and mobile; attempts to fix those images with light-sensitive compounds aimed to record their colors. Prior to the public announcement in 1839 of Louis-Jacques-Mandé Daguerre's daguerreotype process, philosophers, artists, and scientists had long speculated upon the circumstances required to photochemically render the colors of nature. Since various substances changed color when exposed to light, early photochemical experiments generated multiple hues independent of a camera. Failure until the late nineteenth century to secure viable photographic color processes was not owing to a lack of desire for polychrome. Instead, it resulted from an inability to photochemically capture objects in the colors in which they appeared.

The first stable photographic nineteenth-century processes generated monochromatic images; but they were images of various single colors rather than of "black and white" with which monochrome has become synonymous. Monochromatic representation has a complex history. As a recent exhibition at London's National Gallery testified, monochrome was not simply the favored medium for painters' preparatory sketches. Artists used monochrome in many aspects of picture-making and a variety of aesthetic and philosophical motives governed their choice. From antiquity, philosophers debated the practice of using predominantly black and white pigments to differentiate light and shade. Pliny the Elder discusses "monochromaton,"[1] the employment of single colors, in the originary stages of painting. While in the medieval and Renaissance periods, some paintings combined grey scale, or "grisaille" with "polychromy," in other cases monochrome images were "restricted to the margins" or were found, for example, "painted on the reverse" of brightly colored "altarpiece shutters."[2] As monochrome photographs appeared, offering viewers a world akin to that captured by tried and trusted manual processes of reproduction, some reflected upon a de-saturated world in which, in John Ruskin's words, "all flowers were grey, all leaves black, and the sky *brown*."[3]

Although 'black and white' photographs quickly proliferated in communities already attuned to reproductive technologies such as engraving and lithography, the physics as well as the chemistry of early photography was very much concerned with colors. By famously using a glass prism to refract a sunbeam onto the wall of a darkened room, Sir Isaac Newton (1642–1727) had demonstrated, in his *Opticks* of 1704, the rainbow of colors—red, orange, yellow, green, blue, indigo, violet, and their gradations—that comprise white light and form the visible spectrum.[4] Colors, evident in "Newton's Rings," and visible in certain beetles and in soap bubbles, were subsequently understood not as the result of actual pigments, but rather of interference by a thin film around the point of contact of rays of light. Newton had revealed "additive synthesis" as produced by light as distinct from "subtractive synthesis," by which the mixture of colored pigments produced black. As "developed by [Thomas] Young's work, and decisively formulated by James Clerk Maxwell and Hermann von Helmholtz,"[5] Newton's theory led eventually to the "indirect" method of color photography known as trichromy.

Opposed to that of Newton, Johann Wolfgang von Goethe's treatise *Zur Farbenlehre*, published in 1810 and, as *Theory of Colours*, in English in 1840,[6] comprised a physiological account emerging from multiple experiments. Having studied manifestations of colors over many years Goethe put the observing subject's responses at the center of his phenomenological enquiry. As a reminder of the relative permeability of nineteenth-century disciplines, the physicist Thomas Johann Seebeck was closely involved with Goethe's explorations, as scientists worked alongside philosophers, artists, and writers in striving to understand colored images. When Daguerre's revolutionary daguerreotype was publically announced in Paris, he had been seeking to arrest color. To support his earlier invention, the diorama, Daguerre had run a laboratory to experiment with "the chemistry of colours"[7] for scenic effects.

Monochromatic processes, distinct from Daguerre's, evolved simultaneously in many countries. While the most well-known in the British context were William Henry Fox Talbot's "photogenic drawing," followed by his calotype process of 1840, as Ian Jeffrey has indicated, color had been "high on photography's wish list from the very beginning."[8] Although beyond the scope of this largely Victorian study, as evidenced by nineteenth-century Chinese and Japanese hand-coloring, contemporaneous pioneers worldwide regarded color as integral to photographic experimentation.[9] In Europe, while Daguerre's process produced direct positive images on metal, Talbot's calotype generated negative images on paper from which positive salted paper prints could be made. Independently, in France, Hippolyte Bayard invented a direct positive paper based process (Figure 1).[10] But, since it proved impossible for pioneers working in the late 1830s and early 1840s to photochemically fix for any sustained length of time the natural colors of objects, those monochromatic processes of daguerreotype and calotype that quickly caught on embodied elements of compromise.

Histories of photography, however, tend to overlook the enduring interest in color masked by such compromise. Moreover, monochromatic prints were themselves never uniformly black and white. As scholars such as Larry Schaaf[11] have shown, Talbot's photochemical experiments displayed a variety of hues determined by subtle differences in the chemical mixtures and exposure times employed. In Talbot's 1839 photogenic drawing *Leaves of Orchidea* (Plate 1), for example, a translucent network of botanical veins emerges from copper-

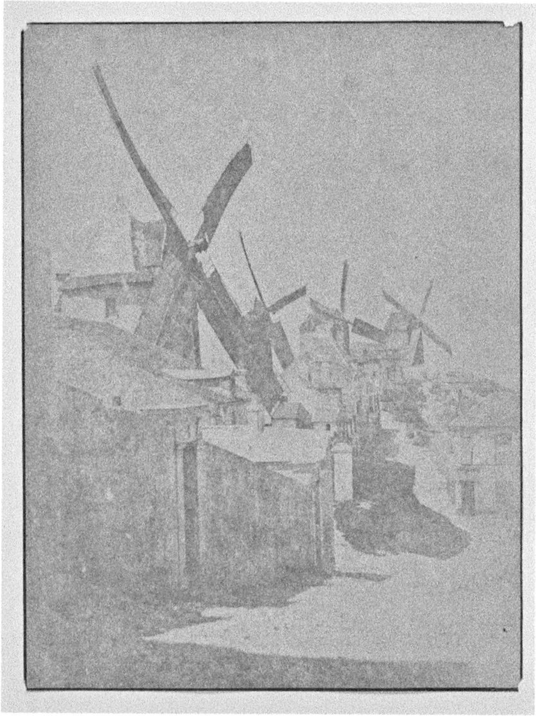

FIGURE 1 Hippolyte Bayard, *Windmills of Monmartre* (1842), salted paper print.

brown tones of the paper. Daguerreotypes on metal, meanwhile, presented unpredictable chromatic effects or irregular shades of coloration. Such variety of hues at the inception of the medium kept alive the future possibility of photographically securing a greater chromatic range. At the same time, by the 1850s, with the introduction of albumen prints, people began to lament the loss of violet and yellow tones captured in the earlier salted papers. Thus, by the mid-century, with increasing standardization of photographic materials and prior to any stable color process, we already witness antipathy toward the "generic brown" of an albumen print "not toned with gold."[12]

As Heinrich Schwarz demonstrates, as a monochromatic technology, photography was not seamlessly accommodated to existing technologies without "the perplexity and the conflicts of contemporary judgements."[13] For Schwarz, the advent of photography generated greater resistance than had that of lithography in 1796.[14] Toward the middle of the eighteenth century, prior to the invention of lithography, print makers had developed several pioneering techniques using color. As Margaret Morgan Grasselli explains, these included new intaglio processes "printed from lines incised or etched into metal plates" such as "color mezzotint, chalk manner, pastel manner, acquatint and wash manner, which were all specifically designed for color printing."[15] While many early woodcuts were hand painted, according to Grasselli, prior to the mid-eighteenth-century boom in the market for color prints, especially in France, color played a relatively marginal role in the history of printmaking.[16]

In the 1690s, Jakob Christoffel Le Blon developed his three-color system by over-printing mezzotint plates registered on white paper. Following Newton's "additive synthesis," Le Blon discovered it was possible to "create virtually the entire spectrum of colour with just three basic hues of ink – blue, red, and yellow – printed one on top of the other from several plates"[17] (Plate 2). His process allowed the "printing" of portraits and oil paintings, he claimed, "with the same precision, same regularity and same exactitude as if they were painted with the brush."[18] Le Blon's process anticipates the reproductive capacities of photography; one of the earliest photographic color processes was a trichromatic one that worked with three plates. Moreover, Le Blon's color process from multiple plates, "by which he had to *estimate* his mezzotint screen values," provides the basis for the halftone color reproduction techniques we use today.[19]

Established forms of color printing preceding the invention of the daguerreotype only highlighted the failure of photography to render objects in color. Popular print-making technologies provided consumers with high-quality colored reproductions. Thus, monochromatic daguerreotypes and calotypes would have initially appeared at a chromatic disadvantage alongside, for example, an exquisitely colored eighteenth-century print such as Jean-François Janinet's *La Toilette de Venus*, after François Boucher (1783) (Figure 2), "in wash manner, printed in green-blue, red, carmine, yellow, and black inks."[20] Later in the mid-nineteenth century, a lack of color in photographs would remain striking. From 1851, monochromatic albumen prints produced by Frederick Scott Archer's wet collodion process presented a very different appearance to chromo-lithographs printed by multiple applications of lithographic stones inked with different colors. Crucially, however, nineteenth-century viewers, long attuned to monochromatic representations, and to applied color in engravings and lithographs, expressed different expectations of photographically generated images. The causal, or indexical, connection of the photographic image to its referent led viewers initially to expect the medium to reproduce objects in the colors in which they were seen. For some, color became the sticking point of a medium widely praised for its unprecedented verisimilitude. As photochemical traces photographs were ontologically different from their antecedents. Such ontological differences, occupying both practitioners and viewers, played out in different ways in the various texts of the period.

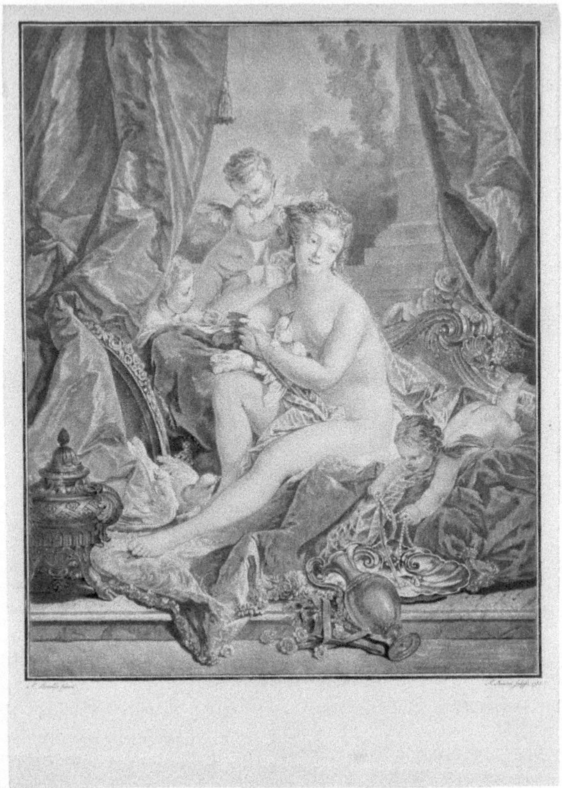

FIGURE 2 Jean-François Janinet, *La Toilette de Venus* after Francois Boucher (1783), etching and wash-manner engraving, printed in color from four plates.

Pigments

For a long time, it was believed that the marble of prized Greek antiquities was pure white. When archaeologists detected vestiges of color upon the surfaces of ancient marbles, viewers refused to accept colored pigments where they believed there to have been none. In the 1830s, for example, most scholars contested Gottfried Semper's view that ancient monuments had originally been polychromatic: "Winckelmann's aesthetics were embraced, and these did not include paint on sculpture."[21] The case of color in nineteenth-century photography requires, metaphorically at least, an analogous process of excavation. For, like such conceptions of Greek sculpture as uniformly white, accounts of early photography often fail to notice instances of color and erroneously accept the medium as fundamentally monochromatic. With similar amnesia regarding color in early photography, the archaeological term "excavation" aptly describes the retrieval of its buried traces.

A mid-nineteenth-century painting by William Dyce newly probes the relationship between the chromatic and the achromatic. But *Titian Preparing to Make his First Lesson in Colouring* (1856–57) (Plate 3)[22] also visualizes the materiality of pigments in painting that cannot be separated from an understanding of the relationship of color to photography. Dyce depicts the boy Titian seated in a garden, contemplating a sculpture of the Madonna and child that he prepares to paint. Cut flowers spill from a basket while a water flask stands ready to dilute their juices for pigments. The concentrated field of polychrome provided by the flowers in an otherwise tonally even painting contrasts strikingly with the whiteness of the statue. Dyce's differentiation of color from black and white engages the place of photography as not yet able to reproduce color.[23] For the monochromatic sculpture that awaits colors from the young Titian's brush conjures "the detachment from life of monochromatic representation"[24] together with contemporaneous mid-nineteenth-century practices of applying color to photographs.

Dyce's depiction of the great Venetian colorist also evokes Sir John Herschel's experiments with organic dyes and a profound sense of the physicality of color as extracted directly from plants. In the earlier historical moment it represents, the painting predicts subsequent chemical fixing of the physical trace, the "photographicness" of photography as a pressed relation to the object rather than simply a method of inscription.[25] Allegorizing the colorist Titian will become, Dyce thereby alludes both to foundational accounts of the origins of color in painting and also to nineteenth-century philosophical and aesthetic questions of color vital to new photographic experiments.[26] Research in chemistry, physics, botany, and astronomy overlapped, often in subtle ways, with developments in engraving, painting, the textile industry, and manufacturing, to contribute to what became known as photography. However, the place of color in photography tends to be separated from wider nineteenth-century interest in the materiality of images and image-making technologies. Yet, to reconsider color in nineteenth-century photography it is necessary to examine changes in the wider cultural significance of color in a period undergoing a revolution in the production of pigments.

The Colours of the Past in Victorian England, edited by Charlotte Ribeyrol, reminds us that the case of color more generally in the nineteenth century is one in which the development of aniline dyes figures large.[27] But not only in a practical and commercial context, for "the transformation of the nature of pigments and dyes by nineteenth-century chemists was equally the object of heated discussion in aesthetic circles."[28] The manufacture of aniline dyes from coal-tar, "devised for an expanding textile industry," had the effect of "de-stabiliz[ing] the terminology of colour,"[29] Ribeyrol notes, to the extent that the writer John Addington Symonds considered "such commercial hues unsuitable for poetic use."[30] Moreover, prominent social commentators of the period,

John Ruskin and William Morris, also registered significant aesthetic losses resulting from a shift from natural mineral pigments and dyes to modern artificial ones. While Ruskin bemoans the modern production of purple from "coal instead of the sea,"[31] for Morris, the antique purple, that "most splendid of colours,"[32] extracted from "the now lost murex or fish-dye" remains only in examples of the "vellum stained purple" of Byzantine books. Ruskin's and Morris's comments on purple are part of a larger response to nineteenth-century transformations in the production of colors that affected both their strength and their permanence. As Ribeyrol writes, new "ready-made" pigments "were deemed more fugitive than their ancient, organic or mineral counterparts."[33]

In the context of photography, however, the color purple—in experiments involving light sensitivity—emerges in pioneering terms in William Cole's "Letter to the Philosophical Society of Oxford: Containing his Observations on the Purple Fish" (1685), published in book form (1689).[34] Cole was a British naturalist and collector who, taking his cue from Pliny the Elder's writing on the production of Tyrian purple[35] from the murex (Figure 3), made empirical experiments with dye extracted from sea snails. Those snails recall the origin story, from Julius Pollux's *Onosmasticon*, of the discovery of the murex by Heracles's dog as depicted by Peter Paul Rubens whose mythological scene pictures the animal with his mouth stained by the purple/red dye (Plate 4).[36] Cole's account of using the dye to mark linen with letters and numbers, invites re-evaluation of the place of color in pre-photographic experiments with pigments and light. Demonstrating the light-sensitivity of the substance extracted from *Purpura lapillus*, he observes the metamorphosis from pale green, through red, to the purple of Pliny's account.

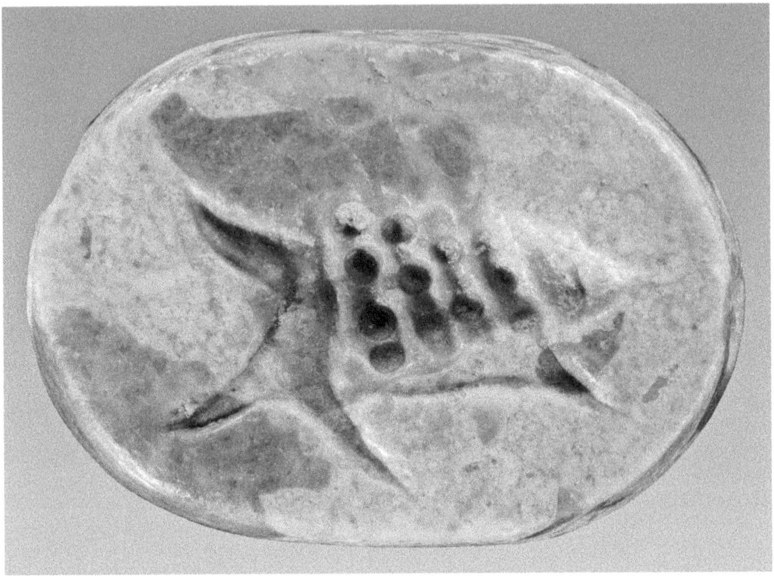

FIGURE 3 Unknown, *Engraved Scaraboid with murex shell*, Greek (about 400 BC), mottled green and yellow jasper.

Cole's fascination lodges in the covert nature of his color source, and in a lack of correspondence between the organic substance employed for dyeing and the polychromatic results obtained. When exposed to the sun, liquid, hidden in "a white vein" of the shell, generates a rainbow of colors. While Rubens depicts Heracles's dog as having bitten into the mollusc to release the prized purple, Cole "digg'[s] it out with the stiff point" of a pencil.[37] Using the dye to add permanent initials to fabrics, the naturalist employs the sun to generate colored letters for purposes of identification. To prevent them from fading, Cole consigns his photochemically produced colors to a book. He thereby approaches the photochemical mark-making of later photographic explorations and, in effect, anticipates the photo-book or album which in modified form will become a popular method of consuming photographs. Cole writes with light to generate vibrant yet ephemeral colors. But he does so, not by blocking solar action later characteristic of the contact print but, instead, by inviting the sun to transform the organic substance of those marks into colored letters. Cole is intrigued by the chemical transformation of one hue into another. But he is also drawn to the "graphy"—or writing—that would come to constitute as vital a component of the nomenclature "photography" as "photos", or light.

Photochemistry

A sense of the fugitive qualities of modern pigments, in the context of Cole's empirically observed organic ones, connects with the equally evanescent nature of the image in early nineteenth-century photochemical research. Humphry Davy's publication in 1802 of an "Account of a Method of Copying Paintings upon Glass" outlines Thomas Wedgwood's experiments with changes in the "colour" of paper and white leather "moistened with solution of nitrate of silver" when exposed to solar rays.[38] Davy observes how the support takes on "different shades of grey and brown, [until] it becomes at length nearly black" and "the alterations of colour take place more speedily in proportion as the light is more intense."[39] Lady Elizabeth Eastlake, in her seminal essay "Photography" (1857), maintains that the significance of Wedgwood's and Davy's aim "lay in the first stain designedly traced upon the prepared substance, not in the thing it portrayed."[40] Differentiating photochemical generation of marks from mimetic images produced in a camera obscura, Eastlake voices the separation of pictorial from photochemical possibilities of the medium.

Photography as imprint is, as Geoffrey Batchen notes, photography "in its most primal state" and, by extension, at its most distinct from forms of mark-making by hand.[41] But photographs as physical imprints further complicate notions of the medium as simply accommodated without question to a monochromatic pictorial tradition. Indeed, Eastlake goes as far as to suggest that in attempting to copy colored glass Wedgwood and Davy were driven by a desire for color.[42] Variations procured with light-sensitive compounds indicated the enticing prospect of fixing color photochemically. Moreover, alert to the presence of color, Wedgwood recognized that to harness polychromatic images by solar light would be precisely to liberate image-making from the realm of pigments, inks and dyes.

"Cloths of Gold"

Following Cole's experiments, and prior to those of Wedgwood and Davy, Elizabeth Fulhame produced pioneering photochemical results with color and textiles. Working in Edinburgh in the 1780s and 1790s, she experimented with the action of light on metal salts to attempt to make "cloths of gold, silver and other metals."[43] Fulhame's experiments generated a range of colors photochemically. Although little is known of her life, not only did Fulhame document her experiments, but, in 1794, she also published a detailed account of them in *An Essay on Combustion, with a view to a New Art of Dying and Painting*. Among other findings, Fulhame discovered the vital role of water in the reduction of metals by light. Yet her work remains largely neglected.[44] That neglect is not simply owing to difficulties in identifying individual contributors from the multiple disciplines from which the potential for photographic images eventually emerged. It also owes much to the fact that Fulhame was female. She was married to the physician Thomas Fulhame who studied chemistry at the University of Edinburgh but, as a woman, Elizabeth Fulhame was denied a university education. At once bold and systematic in her experiments, Fulhame prefaced her treatise with a proto-feminist account of her motivations for publishing it. Her unashamed stance on sexual politics clearly alienated some male readers. It was precisely designed to do so.

Fulhame's publisher was Joseph Johnson, the liberal publisher better known for publishing the work of Thomas Paine, Richard Price, Joseph Priestley, and Mary Wollstonecraft. As Fulhame claims, she published *An Essay on Combustion* to prevent plagiarism by her male contemporaries. While Priestley called her theory "fanciful and fabulous, as the story of the phenix itself,"[45] Fulhame was not wholly dismissed for her radical stance. Her voice resonated for some of her male contemporaries including Count Rumford.[46] The book was republished in Philadelphia in 1810 with a preface lamenting its neglect[47] and Robert Hunt recognized especially Fulhame's identification of the significance of water to the image-forming reaction.[48] Communicating "beautiful and unexpected colours" emerging in her experiments, Fulhame allows us to reassess the evolution of photography as a distinctly colored phenomenon.

The example of Fulhame also focuses the place of gender in this collection and in early photography more generally. While, stories of "great men"—and the equally "great" rivalries among them—have tended to drown out, or assign to the periphery, other voices, Fulhame's work demonstrates women's involvement in photo-chemistry, heralding not only the invention of photography, but also the production of colored images. In conducting her experiments with basic equipment in a domestic context, Fulhame also challenged those borders—later challenged by photographers—separating amateur and professional scientific practice, demonstrating that knowledge was produced and exchanged among individuals and communities whose archives may not have survived, or among those who may not have enjoyed the social status to command an archive. Forcefully addressing gender discrimination, Fulhame's account of chemical generation of color also invites us to reconsider what would later become designated as "photographic."

Anna Atkins (1799–1871),[49] who in the 1840s creatively employed the cyanotype, has only quite recently gained recognition for her pioneering use of the striking monochromatic blue process invented by Sir John Herschel (Plate 5). Atkins arrested images of marine algae and plants, independent of a camera, to produce some of the earliest books of photographs (Plate 6).[50] Her prints, created by the sun's direct contact with specimens laid upon photosensitized paper, are imprints as well as representations. Cyanotypes focus the agency of photography as searing the surface of the support and, as Patrick Maynard and Geoffrey Batchen have shown, they have the capacity to frustrate notions of photography as primarily a pictorial medium.[51] For Carol Mavor, Atkins's *Sea Algae* in "their pools of blue"—resembling the ocean from which the specimens come—"are particularly thalasso-graphic (sea-writing)."[52] In vital ways, too, the monochromatic blue of the cyanotype highlights ways in which a desire for multicolored palettes gave way to various distinctive monochromatic ones.

In 1869, Julia Herschel (1842–1933), daughter of Sir John Herschel, photographed by Julia Margaret Cameron in 1865 (Figure 4), took up

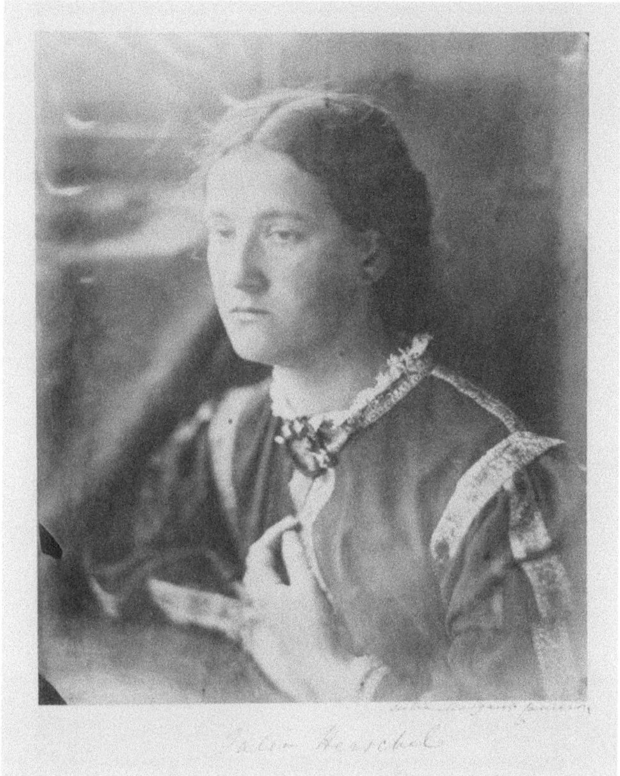

FIGURE 4 Julia Margaret Cameron, *Julia Herschel* (1865), albumen silver print from glass negative.

her father's cyanotype process and, by association, the legacy of Atkins, to publish *A Handbook for Greek and Roman Lace Making* (Figure 5).[53] The volume, which included 22 cyanotypes, represented a significant choice of medium. For, in the 1860s, following advancements in photographic technologies, Julia Herschel selected a process requiring not even a rudimentary camera. While her choice of the cyanotype might appear anachronistic, at a point when it remained prohibitively expensive to include photographs in books, that choice represents a fitting means of capturing tactile qualities of patterns of lace. In

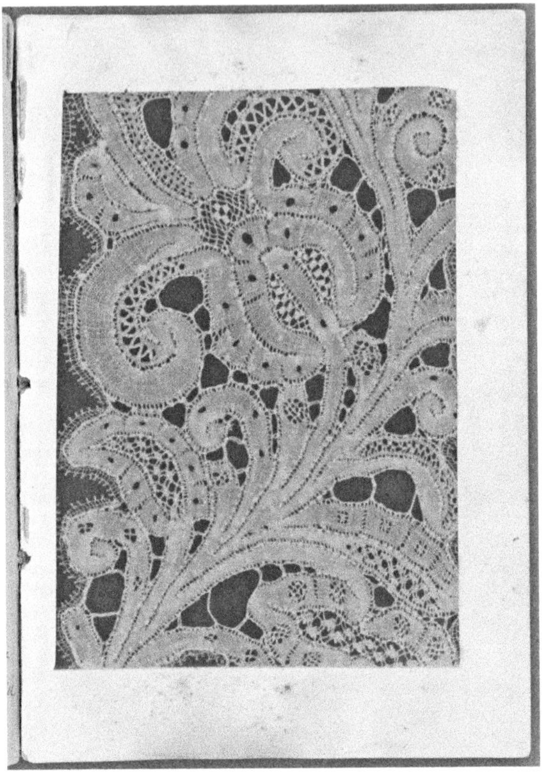

FIGURE 5 Julia Herschel, *Braid and thread lace* (1869), cyanotype.

employing the process, Julia Herschel evokes the haunting registers of earlier cyanotypes such as that of Bayard's sky-blue setting of mottled feathers (Plate 7).

While the cyanotype generated a single color "blue," different colors emerged in trials with contact prints. The chrysotype, for example, invented by Sir John Herschel in 1842, which used light-sensitive iron salts developed with gold chloride solution, generated dark purple hues (Plate 8). Thus, reconsidering such early experiments with color, it is vital to recognize that, in the 1840s, it was not a foregone conclusion that photographic greyscale would become a visual norm. The past might have been otherwise colored. And monochromatic alternatives to "black and white"—such as "blue and white" and "purple and white"—simultaneously preserved ties to the prospect of polychromatic photography.

"Vegetable Photography" and Herschel's "Pink Lady"

Sir John Herschel experimented with preparations of gold, platinum, mercury, iron, and copper, among other metals, to discover they were "more or less sensitive, and capable of producing pictures of beauty and distinctive character."[54] His pioneering work in color and light yielded results equally as fleeting as those of his predecessor Fulhame. Moreover, Herschel acknowledged Fulhame's original research in his 1839 paper to the Royal Society.[55] Records of Herschel's photochemical experiments indicate that the possibility of all manner of colored outcomes for photographic images provided a large part of their magical appeal. In his account of Herschel's chrysotype process, Mike Ware explains how, although "gold was considered as a potential imaging substance" it "failed to compete with silver in photography" because it was expensive and technically difficult to use.[56] Colors produced by the chrysotype were also hard to control and their fluctuations highlight the fleeting nature of early photochemical generation of color. While Herschel's chrysotype was one outcome of a widespread nineteenth-century drive to photochemically arrest color, as Ware indicates, Herschel was especially committed to the different colors generated by plant juices. Between August 1840 and July 1842, Herschel recorded 225 anthotypes (images made using plant dyes) which, as Ware writes, "took considerable effort in preparation and many days of exposure," were "not far behind in number at 314 his experiments with silver," and "dominated" Herschel's 1842 paper."[57] Given such plant juices were less sensitive to light than silver salts, and Herschel was unable "to fix these images," Ware believes Herschel persisted with them owing to their potential for color and to his belief in the possibility of "colour photography."[58]

Herschel's research also testifies more generally to the serendipitous nature of chemical experimentation with color in the period, as when, in a letter of April 6, 1841, he discloses to Talbot that one of his images he thought lost has unexpectedly turned up: "I think I some time last summer sent you a Pink Lady – but it was a bad specimen. That which I meant to have sent was at the time mislaid. Two or three days ago it turned up in the leaves of a book and I now send her for your inspection."[59] This fortuitous discovery prompts Herschel to identify "the juice of the red double stock" as "the colouring matter" that had turned the figure "pink," before noting further that "the most sensitive vegetable matter I have yet met with is the green juice of the red cabbage – the action is very slow – but attended with some curious phenomena."[60]

As letters of the 1840s between Herschel and Talbot further testify, Herschel's pursuit of a direct positive process in natural color, by what he called "vegetable photography," also contributed to a larger discourse of serendipity. For in early photography, things appeared and disappeared. Sometimes they disappeared only to reappear unexpectedly at some later date. Herschel's and Talbot's experiments were frequently attempts to stop the disappearance of a colored image captured on sensitized paper. Or, to prevent the sun from running its course to blackness. Thus, when Herschel, writing to Talbot on March 25, 1843 about his chrysotype process as "a pretty pendant to [Talbot's] Kalotype," encloses examples for his "inspection,"[61] he notes: "I must request their return as they form part of a series, which I keep under my eye to watch their slow changes which are very curious and in some cases end in total or almost total obliteration in others with a most remarkable increase of clearness and distinctness."[62] Here, as elsewhere, we also find evidence of early chemical experimentation as a slow waiting game. Herschel, in the previously cited letter to Talbot of April 6, 1841, reports that the image he calls his "pink lady" had spent "a week and upwards in the Sun"; such was the length of time required to develop a positive impression from an engraving taken on sensitized paper.[63] In histories of photography, evanescence, as initially characteristic of color, becomes subordinate to what will become the relative permanence of monochrome. Yet, the potential for color, only repressed and not forgotten, remained recoverable by various means.

The Sun as Colorist

A sketch by George Cruikshank, accompanying Sidney Laman Blanchard's poem "Photographic Phenomena, or the New School of Portrait-Painting" of 1842, shows a bespectacled figure of the sun, appearing as his namesake flower. Holding out a brush the sun is about to lay color upon the rotund figure of earth positioned beside a comparatively dainty moon:

Apollo turned R. A.
The other day,
Making a most decided hit
They say

ll. 35–38[64]

This sketch of the earth "sitting" to the sun "artist" is one of several nineteenth-century graphic representations that play upon the anthropomorphization of solar rays by photography. Cruikshank's image recalls photographs from the same period that stage the emergence of the photographic medium. Oscar Rejlander's "The Infant Photography Giving the Painter an Additional Brush" (1856) pictures the new medium interacting with the established figure of painting as in possession of a palette of colors. In Julia Margaret Cameron's "Cupid's Pencil of Light" (1870), by contrast, the infant cupid draws upon a dazzling solar tablet.[65] Cruikshank, meanwhile, gives his sun a palette loaded with pigments which might appear somewhat redundant in a period of emerging photographic monochrome. But Blanchard and Cruikshank also raise the topical issue of solar agency and, in the context of early experiments with color, prompt us to further revisit the anthropomorphizing of sunlight. After all, if the sun is doing the work of the artist, then the role of photographer, as conduit for solar light, is also in question.

Anthropomorphization of the sun in the language of early photography has received interesting analysis.[66] But the relationship to color of such anthropomorphization has been neglected. Metaphors of photography as light's brush, or the solar pencil, as enshrined in William Henry Fox Talbot's *The Pencil of Nature*,[67] comprise significant elements of the nineteenth-century vocabulary of the medium. But, as a letter from Herschel to Talbot of August 30, 1840 reveals, in the realm of photographic agency the fundamental question of polychrome is also very much at issue:

> I enclose you a specimen which (the sun being too superb to resist the temptation of trying *once* more for colours) I produced this morning. It holds out I think a very fair promise of solving the problem of coloured Photographs being a faint & rainbow like, but yet unequivocal representation colour for colour of the whole luminous part of the spectrum and what is of no small importance a *positive* one i.e. bright on a dark ground.[68]

Here, Herschel specifically seeks to "solv[e] the problem of" the "faint and rainbow like" appearance of "coloured Photographs." Especially striking is his estimation of the sun as "too superb to resist the temptation of trying" for polychrome. For, Herschel communicates his desires in photochemistry as the desire of the sun to "try" "*once* more for colours." The inference is that this is not the first attempt by the sun for "colours." Accordingly, Herschel frames *his* disappointment at not having previously harnessed color as reciprocally the disappointment of the sun. In an earlier letter to Herschel of April 30 that year, Talbot had identified the "many complicated properties" in the "solar flood of light" "which in a vast majority of instances must remain latent, since most of the rays pass away into space, without meeting with any object."[69] Talbot's recognition of those yet unrealized properties of the sun in his use of the word "latent," a word now indelibly aligned with the photographic image, communicates "hidden" photographic potential in which color is implicated.

Echoing Talbot's sentiment, Henry Morley and William Henry Wills begin their satirical article "Photography" published anonymously in Dickens's *Household Words* in 1853, by pronouncing "light from the sky" as "the chief part of the stock-in-trade of a photographer."[70] Documenting a visit to John Mayall's Regent Street studio, the authors marvel at the economic benefits of an endless supply of sunlight; they go on to note that: "other light than the sun's can be employed; but, while the sun continues to pour down to us a daily flow of light of the best quality, as cheap as health (we will not say cheap as dirt, for dirt is a dear article), sunlight will be consumed by the photographers in preference to any other."[71] Morley and Wills quickly learn that cheap diffused sunlight, via a skylight, is preferable to a directed sunbeam to avoid hard contrasts and strong shadows that will later characterize the "thrown" light of flash. The journalists' subsequent description of watching the making of a daguerreotype anthropomorphizes the "silver" surface "reposing in the darkness" before being "laid open to receive the meditated shock upon its sensibility."[72]

Lady Elizabeth Eastlake identifies the wet collodion process as supplying an element of rapidity that reforms the sun, a former "sluggard," such that he needs but to "wink" his "eye" to capture objects "with a detail and precision beyond all human power."[73] While much of the discourse of early photography is similarly framed around the sun's relative willingness to perform—he gives freely of, or is reluctant to generate, his rays—the conundrum of color also figures in this discourse freighted with solar metaphors. But, to what extent, and in what ways, do possibilities of color affect discussion of the agency of light in photography? For sure, the case of polychrome reintroduces that thorny question of what it is that defines photographic representation and returns us to ontological questions. Color highlights photochemical generation of the image: its indexical relationship to the referent on the one hand, and its reproductive capacity on the other. In this context, we find Eastlake envisaging in anthropomorphic terms the behavior of different colored rays of the spectrum in darkening photo-sensitive surfaces:

> The prepared paper or plate which we put into the camera may be compared to a chaos, without form and void, on which the merest glance of the sun's rays calls up image after image till the fair creation stands revealed: yet not yet revealed in the order in which it met the solar eye, for while some colours have hastened to greet his coming, others have been found slumbering at their posts, and have been left with darkness in their lamps. So impatient have been the blues and violets to perform their tasks upon the recipient plate, that the very substance of the colour has been lost and dissolved in the solar presence; while so laggard have been the reds and yellows and all tints partaking of them, that they have hardly kindled into activity before the light has been withdrawn. Thus it is that the relation of one colour to another is found changed and often reversed, the deepest blue being altered from a dark mass into a light one, and the most golden-yellow from a light body into a dark.[74]

Figuring the response of different wave lengths of light to the photographic "paper or plate," Eastlake, like several of her contemporaries, criticizes the reduction of colors to inaccurate tonal masses, inaccurate in terms of the representation of the polychromatic values of objects in a monochromatic photographic palette. Such distorted tonal values provoke Eastlake to further conclude that photography "must fail, in the rendering of true chiaroscuro, or the true imitation of light and dark."[75]

Hand-Coloring

Many commentators on photography were equally preoccupied by inaccurate translation of the chromatic scale into monochrome. From the 1840s, processes of hand-coloring addressed a lack of polychrome in daguerreotypes, calotypes and in subsequent emerging processes. When, in the previously cited visit to Mayall's studio, journalists Morley and Wills witness a daguerreotype being made, they note the image is "destined to be coloured."[76] The word "destined" denotes the complement of coloration as the appointed fate of the daguerreotype without which it would remain, in certain senses, incomplete. Morley and Wills recount "the colouring room, a tiny closet in which two damsels were busily at work" with "boxes" of color:

> We pointed to a small box labelled "Sky", remarking that the fair painters were magicians, to carry the sky in a wafer-box. To which one of them promptly answered "Yes; and Ogres, too, for that pill-box contains gentlemen's and ladies' 'Flesh.'"[77]

In addition to the comic possibilities of "magicians" and "ogres" deploying respectively "sky" and "flesh," those labelled boxes containing predetermined shades of color further reinforce hand-coloring as a desirable supplement to the sun's sovereign agency. But, why would the sun, with a veritable rainbow at its disposal, require pigments applied by hand to embellish its images? At a fundamental level, by tampering with its physical and chemical origins, hand-coloring a daguerreotype in 1853 appeared extraneous and antithetical to the status of the photographic medium as it was establishing itself in treatises and manuals. At the same time, as evident in an article in *The Literary Gazette* from 1839,[78] early consumers of daguerreotypes, as well as early makers of them, frequently identified the want of color in the image as a major deficiency to be rectified.

Hand-coloring does not feature extensively in studies of color photography which tend to be driven by the evolution of technological processes. Instead, coloring, or tinting, photographs by hand is often separated from discussions of photographic processes, designated, in its best examples, as a minor art form. But what might it mean to separate manuals on the coloring of photographs from technological discussions when the desired commodity of many a consumer was a photograph with color? As evident in nineteenth-century photographic journals, large numbers of sitters were willing to pay photographers extra for hand-colored photographs, and photographers were keen to provide this service. Therefore, it is important to consider demand for hand-coloring in the larger context of photography and color. In the early decades of the medium, with emerging technological developments, the coloring of photographs contributed to a wider discussion of the relative capacities of processes to harness color. It is only by thus reframing in broad terms the relationship of color to photography that nuanced interconnections emerge.

One reason for a tendency to separate hand-coloring from accounts of color photography is that by the 1850s—as identified by Morley and Wills—coloring photographs had become very much the work of women and associated with a degree of vulgarity. Important to the livelihoods of many photographers, hand-coloring was most popularly used in portraits and democratized portraiture in unprecedented ways. Early daguerreotypes were colored using the established skills of miniature painters and there were variations in approach. While, according to Roger Watson and Helen Rappaport, "American daguerreotypes of the 1840s and 1850s were often enhanced by adding small amounts of powdered red pigment to the image on the cheeks and lips of the sitter," English daguerreotypists crafted "quite elaborate additions of colour to the surface of the plate"[79] as evident in this portrait from Richard Beard's studio (Figure 6). From the first, practitioners

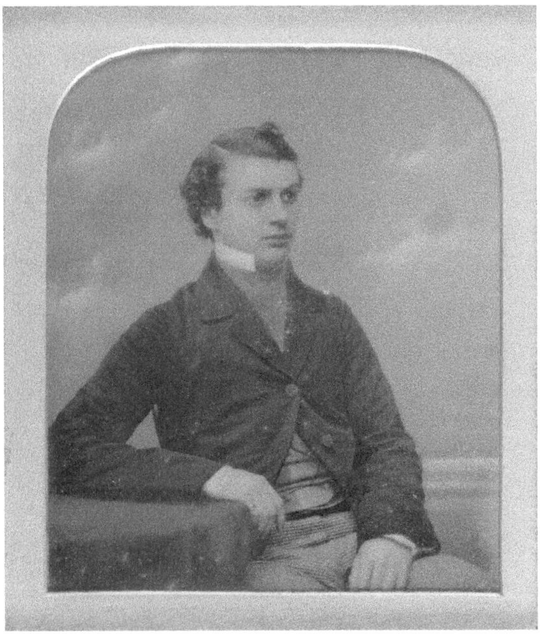

FIGURE 6 Richard Beard, *Portrait of a Young Man Seated at Table* (about 1852), daguerreotype, hand-colored.

foresaw the advantages of hand-coloring and an article entitled "Photographic Portraits" in *Cleave's Penny Gazette* (1842) identifies "the discovery of a method of giving natural colours to the portraits" as "the most important" among "the many valuable improvements recently made in this art."[80] Other commentators denounced standardization as evidenced by rows of ruddy hand-colored faces hanging from the walls of photographic exhibitions. Evident also, in some writing of the period, is a sense that hand-coloring is a form of cheating and a crude relation to pictures produced solely by the sun.

At the same time, the photographic press carried detailed articles on hand-coloring, including a series by Alfred Wall in the *British Journal of Photography* in 1861. Since women performed a significant proportion of hand-coloring, nineteenth-century women's newspapers and magazines provide evidence of its popularity as a profession among them, along with warnings to women about bogus offers of work in photographic coloring. In 1861 *The Lady's Newspaper & Pictorial Times* ran a series of four articles from January to March outlining detailed methods of applying pigments to photographs.[81] In October 1868, "The Englishwoman's Exchange," a section of *The English Woman's Domestic Magazine* facilitating the exchange of goods of all kinds, included the following notice:

> 263. E. M. has a box of photochromy (the art of colouring photographs), only been used once, cost 10s. 6d. She would like in exchange the *Queen* newspaper for 1867, but is open to offers.[82]

One wonders why E. M. did not use the colors more than once and, also, whether she might have connected with a fellow reader, such as Lucy Baird, who had posted in *The English Woman's Domestic*

Magazine the previous year that she "would be glad if any one of the numerous correspondents" would advise "her where she could procure materials for Colouring Photographs, what would be their price, and whether they are difficult to use."[83] Certainly, by the 1860s, dedicated "outfits" for coloring, such as the Newman kit, were readily available, along with instructions for using them.

The hand-coloring of photographs evolved in close relationship to miniature painting. There are several reasons for this connection, not least of which is the easy migration of the fine motor skills of the miniature painter, along with his or her palette of pigments, to the photographic colorist. It is a commonplace that while photography put some miniature painters out of work, others became photographers or colorists. Frequently overlooked, however, are connections between manuals on miniature painting and manuals on coloring photographs as brought together in Section 3. The case of André Léon Larue, known as L. Mansion, is especially interesting since, originally a miniature painter, he became widely celebrated for his virtuosity as a colorist in the Regent Street studio of Antoine-François-Jean Claudet. In 1822 Mansion published his *Letters Upon the Art of Miniature Painting*, detailing all aspects of the process in the form of correspondence with a young woman keen to take up the "art."[84] As early as 1844, Claudet, who had moved from France to England, was tinting and creatively incorporating painted backdrops into his daguerreotypes. Claudet's daguerreotype "Portrait of a Girl in a Blue Dress" (1854) (Plate 9) reveals as integral to the photochemical image what appear to be Mansion's hand-generated tints. The translucent coloring of the child's facial features is exquisite beside the resonant blue of her dress. Yet, her subtle expression is not lost among the red tones of the embossed cushion upon which she leans, nor against the atmospheric perspective of Claudet's pale cerulean sky with tuft of white cloud.

George Thomas Fisher's *Photogenic Manipulation* (1845) singles out Claudet's skills in coloring daguerreotypes and, in 1845, The *Art Union* notes, "no human ever obtained such brilliant effects as these which result from the combined labours of nature and art."[85] This identification of the union of manual labor with the work of the sun also anticipates Eastlake's sentiment that hand-colored portraits represent "a most satisfactory coalition between the artist and the machine."[86] Such "coalition" gains an extra dimension in stereographic form as found, for example, in Claudet's hand-colored daguerreotype of "Boy with a Parrot" (Plate 10) in which the optical resonance of red, blue, and white pigments is doubled. Published anonymously in 1859, *The Principles and Practice of Harmonious Colouring in Oil, Water and Photographic Colours on Paper, Glass and Silver-Plate*[87] reveals a continuum across media in those skills required to produce the miniature forms of portraits. Mansion's advice on meticulous preparation of the miniature ivory surface is not unlike that required for a photograph receiving color. He recommends to his student of miniature painting twelve colors in the flesh palette, enclosing a sample card of those pigments. Mansion later advocates an expanded, palette of fifteen colors for hand-coloring photographs.

A reader of *The English Woman's Domestic Magazine* with the initials F. H. G. enquires in the June 1, 1869 issue about "the best means of preparing photographs for colouring, and also if any handbook of instructions on the art of colouring photographs can be recommended to me."[88] By the late 1860s, along with kits for coloring, there existed a range of such instruction manuals. In addition to texts dedicated to the practice of hand-coloring such as *Harmonious Colouring in Oil, Water, and Photographic Colours* (1859), general photographic manuals, including Marcus Aurelius Root's *The Camera and the Pencil; or the Heliographic Art*, 1864, aimed at an American market, contained at least one section on coloring photographs.[89] Alfred Wall's *A Manual of Artistic Colouring as Applied to Photographs* (1861) advocates the merits of hand-coloring a variety of photographic subjects using "dry or powder colours, watercolours, oils and crayon."[90] But he begins his text by noting the incongruous and "undeservedly questionable" status of colored photographs: "the artist curls his lip at them, because, as *he* says, they are not paintings; and the photographer sneers at them, because, as *he* says, they are not photographs."[91] For Wall, hand-colored photographs divide artist and photographer in telling ways. Such hybrid forms are designated by what they are not. They are "not paintings." Neither are they "photographs." Lamenting the fact that photographic coloring has to "too great an extent fallen into the hands of a class of mechanical daubers, employed because they work cheaply," Wall aspires to divorce hand-coloring from bad taste. To read (in Section 4) Wall's manual in the context of Mansion's text is to newly confront the relationship of the hand to the sun in the larger discourse of photography and color.

In addition to a desire to compensate for absent color in photographs, hand-coloring emerges in nineteenth-century manuals as affecting the permanence of a photograph. In some instances, the application of color was found to preserve the integrity of the photographic image. Consequently, color became connected with pressing anxieties about the fading of photographs, a topic encountered in popular publications and satirized memorably in *Punch* cartoons. In "Photographic Failures" *Punch* (1847),[92] we witness the progressive disappearance across three images of the profile portrait of a male subject. In the final image, all that remains of the supposed photographic likeness are the merest traces of nose, head, and chin. Since, over time, photographs faded or altered in unexpected ways, hand-coloring might be employed to secure elements of the image otherwise permanently lost in the manner envisaged by *Punch*. As Heinz K. and Bridget A. Henisch write, in 1855 the Photographic Society of London set up—in what sounds like a spoof—a "Fading Committee" "charged with the task of identifying causes and recommending remedies for fading."[93] The reasons for photographic fading included "insufficient fixing, insufficient washing after fixing [and] storage under bright light,"[94] and, while, storing photographs in albums might help to delay their disappearance, moisture and acid from album pages presented their own threats to the stability of the image. With no apparent infallible remedy to the problem, adding colors to a photograph might arrest something of an original as it faded. Facilitating an unexpected form of capture, such overlaid color amounted to a type of symbiotic, as well as supplementary, relationship to the photographic image.

Of course, the issue of fading was not unique to photography and had long been a preoccupation of painters. Pliny the Elder describes the ancient Greek painter Protogenes's meticulous application of four layers of paint to his works to attempt to guarantee permanence. As late as 1890, we find William Holman Hunt equally as preoccupied by the potential disappearance of paintings owing to deteriorating modern pigments.[95] In Pliny's story, Protogenes's lack of satisfaction in his depiction of Ialysus, grandson of Apollo, causes the painter to throw his sponge at his painting in frustration.[96] That spontaneous gesture, miraculously generating the colors of nature he had otherwise been unable to simulate manually, powerfully conjures the prospect of automatic color alongside the quest for perfect finish. But the story from *The Natural History* is further relevant to the multifaceted relation of color to photography in the sense that Protogenes's drive to protect an image with successive layers of pigment describes an effect of hand-coloring while predicting, as it were, forms of colored layering that would come to define "indirect methods" of photographic color.

"Indirect" and "Direct" Photographic Color

As the nineteenth century progressed, the problematic of color played out in a range of distinct and overlapping processes and technologies. There were many claims to the status of pioneer of "natural" photographic color. As outlined in Robert Hunt's "On the Application of Science to the Fine and Useful Arts: Heliochrome" (1851)[97] Alexandre-Edmund Becquerel and Niépce de Saint-Victor produced colored images while, in the United States, Levi Hill claimed a unique color process, the Hillotype, documenting at length his evolution as a photographer in *A Treatise on Heliochromy* (1856). Although Hill's claim to have produced daguerreotypes in natural color was quickly discredited, scholars have recently reopened the question of his results after having themselves achieved some success in reproducing them.[98] But it was the Scottish physicist James Clark Maxwell (1831–1879) who, in a public lecture of May 17, 1861, demonstrated what became known as the "three-colour separation process," by which a colored image produced by color selection through filters was generated by superimposing three colored prints.[99] Maxwell's lecture demonstrated Thomas Young's theory that the perception of a variety of colors was owing to the presence of three types of receptors in the eye; each kind being sensitive to one of the three primary colors. As Kim Timby writes, Young had shown how as "the retina deconstructs light, the brain interprets the stimuli it receives to create the variety of colours we perceive";[100] with the help of the photographer Thomas Sutton, Maxwell used three photographs of a tartan ribbon, exposed through red, green, and blue filters, projected on top of one another using three magic lanterns (Plate 11).

Maxwell's full color image made by the brain from three separate primary colored images formed the basis of analogous discoveries. In 1869, Louis Ducos du Hauron and Charles Cros independently submitted to the *Société française de photographie* "additive" or trichromatic screen processes. Ducos du Hauron proposed an "indirect" method of color photography whereby three separate views of an object were taken through different colored filters. He generated a colored image by printing "each negative (with a tinted photosensitive emulsion or with inks) in one of three different colors, superimposing the resulting impressions."[101] Ducos du Hauron's *Still Life with Rooster* (Plate 12) (1869–79) presents a striking taxidermic arrangement. An imposing bird, with splendid plumage and bright red comb, is posed alongside a comparatively diminutive budgerigar with yellow-green plumage. Iridescent veils of color lend a hallucinatory quality to the experience of viewing the polychromatic image.

In addition to such "indirect" methods, a "direct," or "interferential," method of producing color was pioneered by Gabriel Lippmann

(1845–1921), professor of physics at the Sorbonne. Working in the fields of electricity, optics, and thermodynamics, in 1891 Lippmann introduced his process of color photography based on the principle of Newton's rings. As outlined in his lecture to the Royal Society of London in 1896, Lippmann employed a mirror formed by a reservoir of mercury that was positioned to "flow in behind the [photographic] plate,"[102] during exposure and "the effect created by an interval between two reflecting surfaces," "causes the colourless deposit to show bright colours."[103] Situating his method in the context of the history of the problematic of color, Lippmann explains his commitment to a process obviating the need for dyes. Concluding that it is "impossible either to imitate or touch up a colour photograph" produced by his "interferential method,"[104] Lippmann thereby establishes resistance to "touching up" as defining an authentic color photograph.

While Lippmann worked with the principle of "interference," others simultaneously experimented with "indirect" methods of color, using trichromy. Not until the mid-1890s, however, firstly with Frederic Ives's Kromskop system, did color photography using trichromy became commercially available. Ducos du Hauron, in his 1869 submission to the *Société française de photographie*, had suggested an "indirect" method of combining the three primary colors using "a single filter, a three-coloured screen covered either by a thin network of lines, or by a mosaic of dots."[105] But only in 1895 was this process taken up commercially when the Dublin practitioner John Joly employed a screen of fine "closely ruled adjacent lines in orange, green, and violet tints."[106] Kits containing the materials for the process proved popular and several "inventors and manufacturers proposed their own variants and improvements on it."[107] The autochrome, developed in 1904 by

Auguste and Louis Lumière in France, and commercialized in 1907, became the most popular of these variants.

The autochrome process used a screen consisting of "minute grains of starch dyed in red, green and violet (of precisely calculated wavelengths), randomly strewn on a glass plate in the thinnest coat possible."[108] Such arbitrary distribution of the dyed grains lent a singular resonance to the resulting chromatic range, as evident in Auguste and Louis Lumière's "Lilacs" (Plate 13) in which brilliant complementary tones of purple and yellow irradiate the image. While the autochrome simplified processes of color photography—it did not require three individual images, or specialist cameras—it necessitated exposure times of up to thirty times that of a monochrome plate. Moreover, autochrome plates were expensive. Equally significantly, like the daguerreotype, the autochrome was a unique positive (Figure 7) and, as "a coloured transparency on glass," it required projection as a lantern slide, or it might be held up to the light for

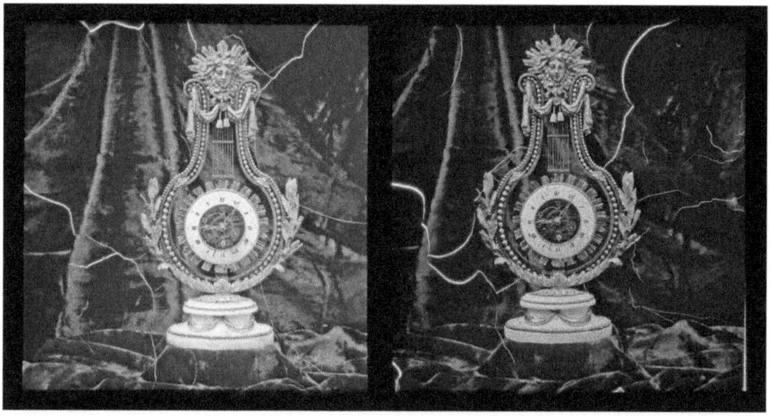

FIGURE 7 Lumière Brothers, *Gold Lyre Table Clock* (about 1898), autochrome, stereograph.

individual viewing, or "seen through a viewer."[109] While it was possible to reproduce an autochrome as a four-color printed illustration, this, too, was a costly process.

As a one-off positive, then, the autochrome presented in some senses a return to the precious unique object of a daguerreotype or, more specifically as a collodion positive on glass, to an ambrotype. In this context, how might we understand the prefix "auto" of autochrome? While autochromes generated "self," or automatic, color of sorts, their polychromatic range depended upon a predetermined placement of colored starch grains. Exposure time determined depth of color, and it was not possible to otherwise adjust or manipulate the colors of the image. This automatism meant that a photographer using the method effectively had to attempt to foresee the eventual distribution of chromatic intensities. The autochrome became the choice of many amateur photographers in the years following its commercialization. While initial interest by established professional photographers and artists was relatively short-lived, amateurs who had attempted earlier more complex color methods took up the process enthusiastically.

One of the earliest exponents of the autochrome in Britain, Sarah Angelina Acland (1849–1900), was an ardent amateur photographer who had earlier worked with what became less well-known color processes. The daughter of Sarah Cotton and Henry Wentworth Acland, friend and colleague of Ruskin, Acland produced pioneering work as detailed by Giles Henderson in *Sarah Angelina Acland, First Lady of Colour Photography, 1849–1930.*[110] Photographed as a child by Lewis Carroll, and involved with Pre-Raphaelite painters, and the photographer Julia Margaret Cameron, Acland took up monochromatic photography in 1891.[111] In 1899 she turned to color, becoming "the leading practitioner of the ground-breaking, but now largely forgotten, 'Sanger Shepherd Process of natural colour photography.'"[112] While *The British Journal of Photography* judged Acland's work "the finest which has ever been publicly shown," as Henderson demonstrates, her achievements in color remain neglected.[113]

It is important to note that Acland's interest in color began with orthochromatic photography, a method of photographic monochrome designed to address the lack of sensitivity of silver salts to the red end of the spectrum. In this regard, Acland approached the problem, earlier identified, of the failure of photographic emulsion to respond to the whole spectrum and the odd tonal values residing in the resulting photographic greyscale. The year 1883 saw the release in Britain of "the first commercial 'orthochromatic' or 'isochromatic' plates" in which "colour sensitizers were added to the emulsion in an attempt to make them responsive to the entire spectrum."[114] In 1895, James William Thomas Cadett (1852–1949) "released the first in a series of 'Cadett Spectrum plates' which, he claimed, were capable of producing 'absolutely correct representation of colour luminosities.'"[115] Acland began her experiments with the Spectrum Plate in 1899, "with daffodils" which, Henderson explains, "were peculiarly revealing of the need for a colour-correct emulsion, their yellow petals and orange trumpets appearing absurdly dark when rendered by ordinary plates."[116] On April 23, 1900, she lectured on Spectrum plates to the Oxford Camera Club, illustrating her talk with lantern slides, ten of which displayed benefits to color photography of the Spectrum plate.[117] Acland's lecture, published that year in the journal *Photography* as "The Spectrum Plate. Theory: Practice: Result," further demonstrated her technical proficiency in the pursuit of color.

After using samples of color slides from Edward Sanger Shepherd for her 1900 lecture, Acland subsequently worked with his method of "Natural Colour" photography. As Henderson notes, the process generated lantern slides to be viewed by hand or by a lantern projector and, therefore, differed from the "Ives colour system" that required "a special viewing instrument."[118] The technically difficult process involved taking three photographic negatives of a subject through red, green, and blue filters from which three positives were printed: "one as a cyanotype on glass, the others on celluloid as magenta and yellow carbon prints" before being "cemented together in 'optical contact' to create a full-colour image."[119] Acland exhibited her first color slides by the Sanger Shepherd method in March 1901; few of them survive. In September 1902, "she became the first woman to show her colour prints on paper at the Royal Photographic Society Exhibition."[120] Later, in 1907, at the Society of Colour Photographers' First Annual Exhibition Acland was praised for avoiding "the common mistake of indulging the appetite for colour to excess."[121] Her subtle effects of color are visible in early prints of Broad Street, Oxford, taken around 1900 (Plate 14 and Figure 8). Produced from three separation glass negatives, the prints capture, from the top of Acland's house, the view across to the corner of Broad Street and Catte Street with the Clarendon building in the right foreground.

Acland's proficiency in multiple color processes, including the more familiar autochrome with which she created a significant body of work, demonstrates how misleading it is to regard the autochrome as the single culmination of a long quest for color. While the autochrome generated singular chromatic effects, the process emerged in a context of overlapping experiments that re-inscribed earlier methods of viewing photographs. Requiring projection, the autochrome recalled

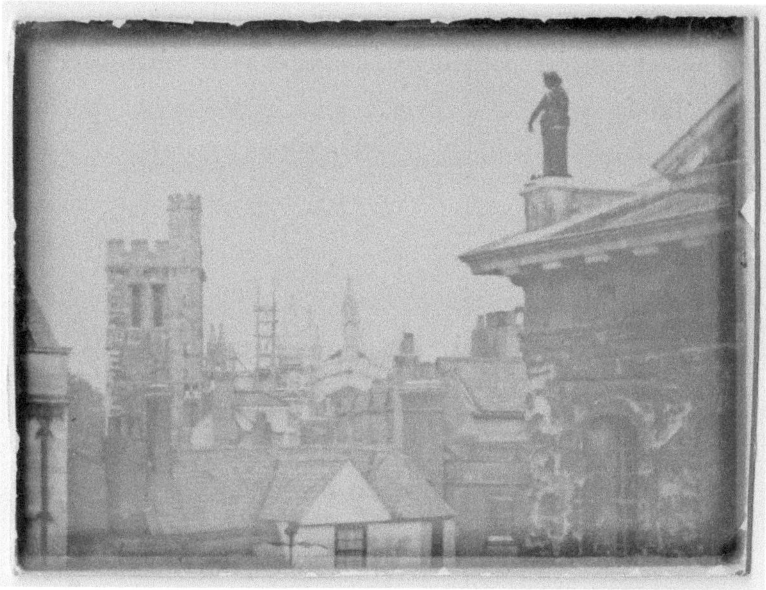

FIGURE 8 Sarah Angelina Acland, *Broad Street, Oxford* (around 1900), color print from three-color separation glass negatives.

the material form of the earlier hand-colored lantern slide. The process did not simply "solve" all the issues that we have been addressing. Indeed, reaction to color following the introduction of the autochrome in 1907 was by no means straightforward.

As the British commercial photographer, and pioneer of color, Madame Yevonde (Yevonde Cumbers) would later note, by the twentieth century veneration of photographic black and white had become so deep-rooted that when, in the 1930s, the Vivex dye transfer process became commercially viable it was greeted with shock. In her autobiography *In Camera*, Yevonde explains that the visual intensity of color was simply too great for photographers, and viewers, educated in a palette of black and white: "they will tell you, quite seriously that the colour photograph is unnecessary and unnatural."[122] Yevonde recognizes that since polychrome appeared supplementary to the photographic image, for those accustomed to a type of seeing through monochrome, acceptance of color photographs would necessitate making strange once more a wholly black and white world. Her portrait "Joan Maude" (Plate 15) realizes Yevonde's claim that a color photograph would make one "stare in amazement at a girl with red hair."[123] Presenting a surfeit of red—in the hair, lips, clothing and backdrop of her sitter—Yevonde conveys the intensity of visual shock long tempered by a naturalization of black and white.

By the time Yevonde was working with color, veneration of black and white had migrated to various forms of "pictorialist" photography developing in part in reaction to color and representing a wish to reclaim the "photographicness" of monochrome. Just as color was marking its presence in photographs, other than by the brush of the colorist, the visual pleasure of monochrome was reasserted as the sovereign domain of "the pencil of nature." In the event, some of those color processes readily embraced by amateurs became again associated with aspects of class and gender prejudice earlier directed at hand colorists. It is not an exaggeration to state that antipathy to polychrome felt by some in the early twentieth century resulted from a belief that "direct" color cheapened the established artistic capacities of photographic monochrome. In the process "black and white" assumed the mantle of "art" photography.

With Color in Mind

In the late twentieth and early twenty-first centuries, with a shift from analogue to digital technologies, color photography remains in the cultural domain of the vernacular. Black and white, by comparison, still occupies the realm of "art" photography. Yet, from the 1970s, some "fine art" photographers began to embrace polychrome; they questioned the relative associations of monochromatic photography with "serious," or professional, uses and color photography with more popular, or amateur, ones. But, still, it did not prove easy to challenge such associations. An interview with the contemporary American photographer William Eggleston in *The Observer* newspaper (2017), for example, reminds us of Henri Cartier-Bresson's negative reaction in the early 1970s to Eggleston's turn from black and white to what would become his signature color.[124] *The New York Times,* meanwhile, had famously pronounced John Szarkowski's 1976 exhibition of Eggleston's photographs at the Museum of Modern Art, New York "the most hated show of the year"; savage responses were directed at Eggleston's saturated color, his "vivid tonal palette and disorienting compositional force."[125]

Eggleston's work was instrumental in the turnaround in attitudes to color from the 1970s; a shift from color considered as a crude relation to the black and white palette, to color as legitimate domain of contemporary "art" photography. Such a shift also represented a radical re-fashioning of a medium that had become associated with working-class tastes, women, and amateur photography. Charlotte Cotton has described unforeseen changes in the market for "photography as art" since the early 2000s when "photography invariably meant coloured Lightjet color prints laminated behind sheets of plexiglass, at least 30 x 40 inches in size."[126] As Cotton writes, "few knew how digital capture or postproduction would impact independent and abstract photography."[127] Such a shift begs the question of the extent of change in the larger cultural positioning of color, a major question beyond the scope of this little book but one emerging from those nineteenth-century material circumstances and aesthetic and technological debates we have engaged. When, in 1976, Eggleston's use of color appeared shocking to a notion of "art" photography, that shock mirrored the response to color earlier identified in the 1930s by Yevonde. Indeed, color created multiple shocks as entrenched twentieth-century objection to polychrome, and preference for monochrome, had endured in part by shrouding a complex nineteenth-century story of color.

Histories of photography remain invested in a narrative of nineteenth-century monochrome in which twentieth-century "direct" color provides a technologically sophisticated breakthrough. The story of photographic color tends to retrospectively imagine early photography from the perspective of a straightforward nineteenth-century naturalization of black and white. While today we experience color as integral to digital photography, we are equally at liberty to drain color from our photographs by switching to black and white. And then, if the whim takes us, to switch back to color, or, radically manipulate its hues. As I write, Brazilian "colorist" Marina Amaral is using Photoshop to digitally "colorize" "old" black and white photographs.[128] Employing layers, she aims to match her colors to those she believes would have been the colors of people and things in a monochrome photograph.[129] Amaral is not alone. Wolfgang Wild and Jordan Lloyd, Sanna Dullaway and Dana Keller, among others, seek to digitally recreate colors of the past.[130] Photoshop is, as Keller explains, "at the core" of his attempt to "bring back" those "things that go unnoticed in greyscale."[131] For Dullaway, colorizing allows "old photos" to be "rescued from the ravages of time," while Wild and Lloyd describe their colorized photographs as "thoroughly restored."[132] The word "restore"—meaning to "repair," or "bring back" to a former state—is telling. Such digital colorizing is not akin to restoring the colors of a painting. For, that which is "restored" in Photoshop never existed in the image. Thus, as colorization aims to reinstate colors with "historical accuracy," it can only hope to simulate the polychrome of objects in the world whose colors always already eluded the monochromatic photographs in which they were captured. Twenty-first-century colorization does not involve pigments and chemicals. Its business is not material color as physically imprinted upon photographic emulsion but color as digitally overlaid. In this sense, colorization compromises Roland Barthes's delight in the knowledge that "the thing of the past" by its "immediate radiations (its luminances), has really touched the surface which in its turn my gaze will touch."[133] Moreover, the digital process recalls Barthes's sense of color as "a coating applied *later on* to the original truth of the black-and-white photograph."[134]

Remembering the colors of the present of a photographic image, in the recent past of its taking, nineteenth-century commentators regularly noted the shortcomings of monochromatic photography in depicting people and things in the hues in which they encountered them. Yet, they kept colors in mind and saw them in "black and white" photographs, anticipating Wittgenstein's seeing through the achromatic—the "lighter or darker grey" scale of a monochromatic photograph—to the chromatic relations it translated.[135] In bringing together the current texts I hope to recall the enduring presence of color both before, and after, that sixty-five-year period between the announcement of the daguerreotype and the availability of autochrome plates. But I also hope to remember a certain "forgetting" of color: a forgetting, that is, in the sense of a marginalization of color in stories of Victorian photography. As we have found, the prospect of harnessing color was not simply eclipsed from 1839 once monochromatic photography entered the public domain. As color endured as a goal of experimentation, it also remained latent in various achromatic hues of early photographs. Moreover, since the indexical nature of a photograph raised a different relationship to absent polychrome from long-established forms of monochromatic representation, nineteenth-century viewers had to newly accommodate themselves to *its* peculiar "black and white." The very non-correspondence of photographic monochromatic tones to the colors they stood in for—the fact, for example, that "orange colour for certain optical reasons" was "photographically black"[136]—highlights the almost alchemical transformations of colors. As this collection demonstrates, Victorian viewers of photographs forgot neither the rich material, nor the diverse conceptual, lives of colors. When not visibly evident in nineteenth-century monochromatic photography, polychrome was only variously buried to remain perpetually available for excavation in the memory.

Notes

1 Pliny the Elder, *The Natural History*, trans. John Bostock and H. T. Riley (London: Taylor & Francis, 1855), Book 35, Chapter 2.

2 Lelia Packer and Jennifer Sliwka, *Monochrome, Painting in Black and White* (London: National Gallery, 2017), 19.

3 John Ruskin, *The Complete Works of John Ruskin*, ed. E. T. Cook and A. Wedderburn, 39 vols. (London: George Allen, 1903–12), VI, 68.

4 Sir Isaac Newton, *Opticks: or a Treatise on the Reflections, Refractions, Inflections and Colours of Light*, 3rd ed. (London: William & John Innys, 1721).

5 Ariane Isler-de Jongh, "The Origins of Colour Photography," *History of Photography*, 18, no. 2 (Summer 1994): 111–119: 112.

6 Johann Wolfgang von Goethe, *Theory of Colours*, trans. Charles Eastlake (London: John Murray, 1840). See Alexanda Loske, *Color. A Visual History from Newton to Modern Color Matching Guides* (Washington, DC: Smithsonian Books, 2019).

7 Steffen Siegal, *First Exposures: Writings from the Beginnings of Photography* (Los Angeles: Getty Publications, 2017), 19.

8 Ian Jeffrey, *Photography: A Concise History* (London: Thames & Hudson), 77.

9 See, for example: Luke Gartlan and Roberta Wue, *Portraiture and Early Studio Photography in China and Japan* (London: Routledge, 2017); Terry Bennett, *Photography in Japan 1853–1912* (Tokyo: Tuttle Publishing, 2006).

10 See Andre Jammes and Eugenia Janis, *The Art of the French Calotype* (Princeton: Princeton University Press, 1983).

11 Larry Schaaf, *Out of the Shadows: Herschel, Talbot and the Invention of Photography* (New Haven: Yale University Press, 1992). See also: foxtalbot.bodleian.ox.ac.uk

12 See Hope Kingsley, "Round Table Two," *Salt & Silver, Early Photography 1840–1860, from the Wilson Collection* (London: Tate, 2015), 59.

13 Heinrich Schwarz, *Art and Photography: Forerunners and Influences* (Chicago: University of Chicago Press, 1987), 90.

14 Ibid.

15 Margaret Morgan Grasselli, *Colourful Impressions: The Print Making Revolution in Eighteenth-Century France* (Washington, DC: National Gallery of Art, 2003), 1.

16 Ibid., 7.

17 Ibid., vii.

18 R. M. Burch, *Colour Printing and Colour Printers* (New York: The Baker & Taylor Co., 1910), xii.

19 Grasselli, *Colourful Impressions*, 42.

20 Ibid., 100.

21 Johannes Siapkas and Lena Sjogren, *Displaying the Ideals of Antiquity, the Petrified Gaze* (New York: Routledge, 2014), 186.

22 William Dyce, *Titian Preparing to Make his First Lesson in Colouring* (Aberdeen: Aberdeen Art Gallery and Museums).

23 Lindsay Smith, "'Thinking Blues': The Memory of Colour in Nineteenth-Century Photography," in *Transactions and Encounters: Science and Culture in the Nineteenth Century*, ed. Roger Luckhurst and Josephine McDonagh (Manchester: Manchester University Press, 2002), 56.

24 Ibid., 59.

25 Ibid.

26 Ibid.

27 Charlotte Ribeyrol, ed. *The Colours of the Past in Victorian England* (Bern: Peter Lang, 2016).

28 Ibid., 8.

29 Ibid.

30 Ibid.

31 Ibid., 15.

32 William Morris, *Hopes and Fears for Art* (London: Ellis & White, 1882), 41.

33 Ribeyrol, *The Colours of the Past*, 11.

34 William Cole, "A Letter from Mr. William Cole, member of Bristol, to the Philosophical Society of Oxford: containing his observations on the purple fish," *Philosophical Transactions of the Royal Society*, 15 (1685): 1278–1286; *Purperea Anglicana, being a discovery of a shell-fish found on the shores of the Severn* (1689).

35 Pliny, *The Natural History*, Book 35, Ch. 26.

36 Peter Paul Rubens, *Heracles's Dog Discovers the Purple Dye*, 1636, Musée Bonnat, Bayonne.

37 Cole, "A Letter from Mr William Cole," 1280.

38 *The Collected Works of Sir Humphry Davy*, ed. by his brother John Davy, Vol. II Early Miscellaneous Papers (London: Smith, Elder & Co., 1839), 240–245.

39 Ibid., 240–241.

40 Lady Elizabeth Eastlake, "Photography," published anonymously, *The Quarterly Review*, 1857, 442–468: 444.

41 Geoffrey Batchen, *Emanations: the Art of the Cameraless Photograph* (Munich: Prestel, 2016), 6.

42 Eastlake, "Photography," 44.

43 Elizabeth Fulhame, *An Essay on Combustion, with a view to a New Art of Dying and Painting* (London: J. Cooper, 1794).

44 Fulhame, *An Essay on Combustion*. Larry Schaaf has identified the importance to photography of Fulhame's treatise. See: "The First Fifty Years of British Photography: 1794–1844," in Michael Pritchard, ed., *Technology and Art: the Birth and Early Years of Photography* (Bath: Royal Photographic Society, 1990), 9–18; *Sun Gardens: Cyanotypes* by Anna Atkins (New York: Aperture, 1985), 23, 100.

45 Derek A. Davenport and Kathleen M. Ireland, "The Ingenious, Lively and Celebrated Mrs. Fulhame and the Dyer's Hand," *Bulletin History of Chemistry*, 5 (1989): 37.

46 Ibid.

47 *Mrs. Fulhame, An Essay on Combustion* (Philadelphia: James Humphreys, 1810).

48 Robert Hunt, *A Manual of Photography*, 3rd ed. enlarged (London: John Joseph Griffin and Co., 1853), 92.

49 A. A. (Anna) Atkins, *Photographs of British Algae: Cyanotype Impressions*, 3 vols. (Halstead Place, Sevenoaks: privately published 1843–1853).

50 See Schaaf, *Sun Gardens*, 23, 100; Lindsay Smith, *The Politics of Focus: Women, Children and Nineteenth Century Photography* (Manchester: Manchester University Press, 1998), 53–55; Carol Armstrong and Catherine De Zegher, eds., *Ocean Flowers: Impressions from Nature* (Princeton: Princeton University Press, 2004).

51 Patrick Maynard, "Talbot's Technologies: Photographic Depiction, Detection, and Reproduction," *Journal of Aesthetics and Art Criticism*, 47, no. 3 (Summer 1989): 263–276, and Batchen, *Emanations*.

52 Carol Mavor, *Blue Mythologies, Reflections on a Colour* (London: Reaktion, 2013), 90.

53 Julia Herschel, *A Handbook for Greek and Roman Lace Making* (London: R. Barrett & Sons, 1869).

54 Eastlake, "Photography," 52.

55 Sir John F. W. Herschel, "Note on the Art of Photography, or the Application of the Chemical Rays of Light to the Purposes of Pictorial Representation," [abstract] *Proceedings of the Royal Society*, 4: 37 (1839), 131–133. The full paper was withdrawn but see the transcript discovered by Schaaf, "Sir John Herschel's 1839 Royal Society Paper on Photography," *History of Photography*, 3, no. 1 (1979): 47–60.

56 Mike Ware, "Herschel's Chrysotype: A Golden Legend re-told," *History of Photography*, 30, no. 1 (Spring 2006): 1.

57 Ibid., 4.

58 Ibid., 4–5. Herschel's search for a direct positive-working process in natural colors was to prove fruitless, as he admitted retrospectively in 1866.

59 *The Correspondence of William Henry Fox Talbot*, foxtalbot.dmu.ac.uk, document no: 4236.

60 Ibid., doc. no.: 4236.

61 Ibid., doc. no.: 4778.

62 Ibid., doc. no.: 4778.

63 Ibid., doc. no.: 4236.

64 *George Cruikshank's Omnibus, Illustrated with one hundred engravings*, ed. Samuel Laman Blanchard (London, 1842), 29–32.

65 Oscar Rejlander, "The Infant Photography" (1856), J. Paul Getty Museum; Julia Margaret Cameron, "Cupid's Pencil of Light" (1870), the Royal Photographic Society Collection.

66 See especially: Joel Snyder, "*Res Ipsa Loquitur*," in Lorraine Daston, ed., *Things that Talk, Object Lessons from Art and Science* (New York: Zone Books, 2004), 195–220.

67 Talbot, *The Pencil of Nature*, first published in 1844–1846 in six separate fascicles.

68 *Talbot Correspondence*, doc. no.: 4129.

69 Ibid., doc. no.: 4070.

70 Morley and Wills, "Photography," *Household Words*, March 19 (1853): 54–61, 55.

71 Ibid., 55.

72 Ibid., 58.

73 Eastlake, "Photography," 52.

74 Ibid., 57.

75 Ibid.

76 "Photography," *Household Words*, 58.

77 Ibid., 58–59.

78 "French Discovery – Pencil of Nature, from 'The New Art,'" *The Literary Gazette*, issue 1150 (February 2, 1839): 74. Equally, color emerges as having the potential to outwit the reproductive capacity of photography. See "Busy with the Photograph," *Household Words*, 9, no. 214 (April 29, 1854): 242–245, in which to prevent forgery it is proposed to print bank notes in "colours, and so beyond the reach of the photograph to imitate."

79 Roger Watson and Helen Rappaport, *Capturing the Light* (London: Macmillan, 2013), 233–234.

80 *Cleave's Penny Gazette of Variety and Amusement*, May 14 (1842), issue 31.

81 *The Lady's Newspaper & Pictorial Times*, "Colouring Photographs. –No. I." (London), Saturday January 31, 1863, issue 840, 244–245.

82 *The English Woman's Domestic Magazine*, Thursday October 1, 1868, vol. v, issue 46, 169.

83 Ibid., Thursday October 1, 1867, vol. iii, issue 34, 560.

84 L. Mansion, *Letters Upon the Art of Miniature Painting* (London: R. Ackerman, 1822).

85 George Thomas Fisher, *Photogenic Manipulation: containing Plain Instructions. Illustrated by woodcuts* (London: George Knight & Sons, 1843), 43; *The Art Union*, June 1, 1845, 171.

86 Eastlake, "Photography," 67.

87 *The Principles and Practice of Harmonious Colouring in Oil, Water and Photographic Colours on Paper, Glass and Silver-Plate, by an Artist Photographer* (London: Cassell, Petter & Galpin, 1859).

88 *The English Woman's Domestic Magazine*, June 1, 1869, issue 54, 325.

89 Marcus Aurelius Root, *The Camera and the Pencil; or the Heliographic Art*, (Philadelphia, New York, 1864).

90 Alfred Wall, *A Manual of Artistic Colouring as Applied to Photographs: A Practical Guide to Artists and Photographers* (London: Thomas Piper, 1861).

91 Ibid., 3.

92 "Photographic Failures," *Punch*, 12, no. 299 (April 3, 1847): 143.

93 Heinz K. and Bridget A. Henisch, *The Painted Photograph 1839–1914, Origins, Techniques, Aspirations* (Pennsylvania: Penn State University Press, 1996), 11.

94 Heinz and Henisch, *The Painted Photograph*, 11.

95 William Holman Hunt, "Address to the London Society of Arts," *Journal of the Society of Arts*, April 23 (1880): 485-499.

96 Pliny the Elder, *The Natural History*, Book 35, Chapter 36.

97 Robert Hunt, "On the Application of Science to the Fine and Useful Arts," *The Art Journal*, October (1851): 257–258.

98 L. L. Hill, *A Treatise on Heliochromy; or the production of Pictures, by means of Light in Natural Colours* (New York: Robinson & Caswell, 1856). In 2007 the Smithsonian's National Museum of American History established that some of Hill's extant "heliochromes" "display natural colours."

99 *Proceedings of the Royal Institution of Great Britain*, 3 (1861), 370–374. See: W. D. Niven, ed., *The Scientific Letters and papers of James Clerk Maxwell* (Cambridge: Cambridge University Press, 1890), 136–137, and Jordi Cat, *Maxwell, Sutton, and the Birth of Colour Photography* (Basingstoke: Palgrave, 2013).

100 Kim Timby, "Colour Photography and Stereoscopy: Parallel Histories," *History of Photography*, 29, no. 2 (Summer 2005): 185.

101 Ibid., 186. For an English translation of Ducos du Hauron's *Les Couleurs en Photographie: Solution du Problème* (Paris: A. Marion, 1870), see Philip Hyper, "Colours in Photography the Problem Resolved," *History of Photography*, 23, no. 3 (Autumn 1999): 281–293.

102 Gabriel Lippmann, "Colour Photography," *Nature*, 53, no. 1383 (April 30, 1896): 617–618, 617.

103 Ibid., 617.

104 Ibid., 618.

105 Isler-de-Jongh, "The Origins of Colour Photography," 111.

106 John Joly, "On a Method of Photography in Natural Colours," *The British Journal of Photography*, 42, no. 11857 (December 6, 1895): 776.

107 Timby, "Colour Photography and Stereoscopy," 192.

108 Isler-de-Jongh, "The Origins of Colour Photography," 115.

109 Ian Jeffrey, *Revisions; an Alternative History of Photography* (Bradford: National Museum of Photography, Film and Television, 1999), 77–78.

110 Giles Henderson, *Sarah Angelina Acland, First Lady of Colour Photography, 1849–1930* (Oxford: Bodleian Library, 2012).

111 Ibid., 10.

112 Ibid., 9–10.

113 Ibid., 10.

114 Ibid., 30.

115 Ibid.

116 Ibid.

117 Ibid, 32.

118 Ibid.

119 Ibid., 33. Henderson explains (36) how the Sanger Shepherd process, using a normal "bellows," or a "repeating back" camera, was "widely practised in the seven years before the Autochrome."

120 Ibid., 34.

121 Ibid., 236.

122 Yevonde, *In Camera* (The Woman's Book Club: London, 1940), 184–187.

123 Ibid., 184.

124 Sean O'Hagan, "The Music's Here then It's Gone Like a Dream," *Observer*, November 19, 2017: 7.

125 Ibid.

126 Charlotte Cotton, "Nine Years, a Million Conceptual Miles," www.aperture.org/magazine-2013

127 Ibid.

128 Marina Amaral, www.marinamaral.com

129 Ibid.

130 See: Wolfgang Wild and Jordan Lloyd, *History as They Saw It: Iconic Moments from the Past in Color* (San Francisco: Chronicle Books, 2018);

Sanna Dullaway, www.sannadullaway.com/about Dana Keller, "Dana Keller Colorizer," www.petapixel.com/201

131 Keller, "My Photo-Shop Story," www.petapixel.com/201

132 Dullaway, www.sannadullaway.com/about; Wild and Lloyd, *History as They Saw It.*

133 Roland Barthes, *Camera Lucida: Reflections on Photography*, trans. Richard Howard (New York: Hill and Wang, 1981), 81.

134 Ibid.

135 Ludwig Wittgenstein, *Remarks on Colour*, ed. G. E. M. Anscombe, trans. Linda McAlister and Margaret Schattle (Berkeley: University of California Press, 1978), section 117: 31e.

136 "Those Who Live in Glass Houses," *All the Year Round*, vol. XII, no. 292 (November 26, 1864): 372–274, 372.

A Note on the Texts

As *Color and Victorian Photography* re-situates the case of polychrome in the context of the emergence and development of nineteenth-century photography, rather than prioritizing the invention of color photography per se, it places neglected texts alongside seminal ones, and alongside texts less obviously "photographic" in their focus.

In Section 1, extracts from J. C. Le Blon's *Il Coloritto* (1720), Goethe's *Theory of Colours* (1820), and Ruskin's *Modern Painters IV* address benefits and shortcomings of monochrome in the context of responses from *The Literary Gazette* to a lack of color in early photographs, and from essays by Antoine Claudet and Charles Martel. Section 2, exploring photochemical experiments, situates extracts from Elizabeth Fulhame's *An Essay on Combustion, with a view to a New Art of Dying and Painting* (1724) alongside Humphry Davy's "An Account of Copying Paintings upon Glass" (1802) and extracts from Sir John Herschel's "On the Action of the Rays of the Solar Spectrum on Vegetable Colours" (1842). Section 3 focuses upon the color purple in texts by William Cole, John Ruskin and from the *British Journal of Photography*, while Section 4 brings together Pliny on Protogenes, L. Mansion's *Letters Upon the Art of Miniature Painting* (1822) and

Alfred Wall's *A Manual of Artist Colouring as Applied to Photographs* (1861) in relation to articles from the journal *Household Words* and *The Lady's Newspaper*. Assessing "direct" and "indirect" color in texts by Robert Hunt, Gabriel Lippmann, Sarah Angelina Acland, and Yevonde, Section 5 also considers, from *All the Year Round* (1864), colors worn by a photographic sitter.

With diverse voices engaged in new conversations, this collection explores color beyond the boundaries frequently allocated to it in early photography. While a chronology of photographic "color processes" emerges, it does so obliquely in thematically grouped texts, some of which pre-date both experiments in color photography and the invention of photography itself.

SECTION 1

"IN TRACES REPRESENTED BY TINTS": MONOCHROME/ POLYCHROME

1

Coloritto or the Harmony of Colouring in Painting

J. C. Le Blon

I.

Of Preliminaries.

Coloritto – or the *Harmony* of Colouring, is the *Art* of Mixing COLOURS, in order to represent naturally, in all Degrees of *painted* Light and Shade, the same FLESH, or the Colour of any Object, that is represented in the true or *pure* Light.

PAINTING can represent all *visible* Objects, with three Colours, *Yellow*, *Red*, and *Blue*; for all other Colours can be compos'd of these *Three*, which I call *Primitive*; for Example.

Yellow and *Red*	}	make an *Orange Colour*.

Red and *Blue* } make a *Purple* and *Violet Colour*

Blue and *Yellow* } make a *Green Colour*

And a *Mixture* of those *Three* Original Colours makes a *Black*, and all *other* Colours whatsoever; as I have demonstrated by my Invention of *Printing* Pictures *and* Figures *with their* natural Colours.

I am only speaking of *Material* Colours, or those used by *Painters*; for a *Mixture* of *all* the primitive *impalpable* Colours, that cannot be felt, will not produce *Black*, but the very Contrary, *White*; as the Great Sir ISAAC NEWTON has demonstrated in his Opticks.

White, is a Concentering, or an *Excess* of Lights.

Black, is a deep Hiding, or *Privation* of Lights.

But both are the Produce of all the Primitive Colours compounded or mixed together; the one by *Impalpable* Colours, and the other by *Material* Colours.

True PAINTING represents

1. Lights by *White*.
2. Shades by *Black*.
3. Reflexions by *Yellow*.
4. Turnings of by *Blue*.

N.B. In Nature, the *general Reflex*-Colour is *Yellow*; but all the *accidental* Reflexions, caused by an opposite Body or Object, partake of the Colour of the opposite Body that caused them.

When a Painter says that such Artists make a good *Coloritto*, he means that they represent truly and naturally the Nude or the naked human Flesh; supposing they can paint all other visible Objects well, and without Difficulty.

In order to learn to paint a good Nude, or any other colour'd Object, we must first learn to represent a white Object. For Example, To paint or represent a Head of Plaister, &c. in which the White will serve to represent the Lights; and the Black the Shades: But White and Black are not alone sufficient to represent like Nature itself, a white Object, which indeed represents a Print or a Design, but not a white Object.

To represent such a white Object, we must add to the Shades, or join with them the Reflex, or the Colour of the Reflex, *viz.* the Yellow; and with the Turnings off, or Roundings, we must join the Colour of the Turnings, *viz.* the Blue. See *Fig.* II.

Only remember, that in natural Objects the Turnings off, or Roundings, are almost imperceptible.

To represent a colour'd Object, we may take an Head of Plaister stain'd with the Colour of Flesh, and set it in a good Light; and then we shall see that the same Colour of Flesh discovers itself throughout, or over all the Head, and distinctly enough, even in the Shades, in the Demishades or Mezzotintaes, in the Reflexions, in the Turnings off or Roundings, &c. [. . .]

II.

To *attain* the Practical Point.

We must know the Difference between the Words *Tincture* and *Colour*, and how these Terms are used.

1. TINCTURE is a liquid Colour, transparent; or (to speak better) a Colour that *conceals* nothing; as the colours in *Dyes* made by Dyers, which hide not the Bodies that are colour'd and cover'd by 'em.

2. COLOUR, in the Practical Part of Painting, call'd a *material* Colour, is a *corporeal* Colour, that comprehends within itself a Body, which hides every thing that is cover'd with it. Yet, there are some colours so *moist*, so transparent, and so little *covering*, that they may be almost reckon'd, or ranked, among the *Tinctures*; such as *Lacca* or *Lack*, *Pink*, *Indigo*, the *Black of Ivory*, &c. notwithstanding they are *corporeal* Colours, as well as the others that *Painters* make use of.

Nevertheless, every *material* Colour is also call'd a *Tincture*, when 'tis us'd to dye *White*, for the representing of *Light*, or the illuminated Parts of an Object.

From: J. C. Le Blon, 1667–1741, *Coloritto or the Harmony of Colouring in Painting, Reduced to Mechanical Practice, under easy precepts, and infallible Rules* (London: 1720), 6–10.

2

Theory of Colours

Johann Wolfgang von Goethe

Chiaro-scuro

849

We apply the term chiararo-scuro (Helldunkel) to the appearance of material objects when the mere effect produced on them by light and shade is considered.

850

In a narrower sense a mass of shadow lighted by reflexes is often thus designated; but we here use the expression in its first and most general sense.

851

The separation of light and dark from all appearance of colour is possible and necessary. The artist will solve the mystery of imitation sooner by first considering light and dark independently of colour, and making himself acquainted with it in its whole extent.

852

Chiaro-scuro exhibits the substance as substance, inasmuch as light and shade inform us as to degrees of density.

853

We have here to consider the highest light, the middle tint, and the shadow, and in the last the shadow of the object itself, the shadow it casts on other objects, and the illumined shadow or reflexion.

854

The globe is well adapted for the general exemplification of the nature of chiaro-scuro, but it is not altogether sufficient. The softened unity of such complete rotundity tends to the vapoury, and in order to serve as a principle for the effects of art, it should be composed of plane surfaces, so as to define the gradations more.

855

The Italians call this manner "il piazzoso;" in German it might be called "das Flächenhafte." If, therefore, the sphere is a perfect example of natural chiaro-scuro, a polygon would exhibit the artist-like treatment in which all kinds of lights, half-lights, shadows, and reflexions, would be appreciable.

856

The bunch of grapes is recognised as a good example of a picturesque completeness in chiaro-scuro, the more so as it is fitted, from its form, to represent a principal group; but it is only available for the master who can see in it what he has the power of producing.

857

In order to make the first idea intelligible to the beginner, (for it is difficult to consider it abstractedly even in a polygon) we may take a cube, the three sides of which that are seen represent the light, the middle tint, and the shadow in distinct order.

858

To proceed again to the chiaro-scuro of a more complicated figure, we might select the example of an open book, which presents a greater diversity.

859

We find the antique statues of the best time treated very much with reference to these effects. The parts intended to receive the light are wrought with simplicity, the portion originally in shade is, on the other hand, in more distinct surfaces to make them susceptible of a variety of reflexions; here the example of the polygon will be remembered.

860

The pictures of Herculaneum and the Aldo-brandini marriage are examples of antique painting in the same style.

861

Modern examples may be found in single figures by Raphael, in entire works by Coreggio, and also by the Flemish masters, especially Rubens.

TENDENCY TO COLOUR

862

A picture in black and white seldom makes its appearance; some works of Polidoro are examples of this kind of art. Such works, in-asmuch as they can attain form and keeping, are estimable, but they have little attraction for the eye, since their very existence supposes a violent abstraction.

863

If the artist abandons himself to his feeling, colour presently announces itself. Black no sooner inclines to blue than the eye demands yellow, which the artist instinctively modifies, and introduces partly pure in the light, partly reddened and subdued as brown, in the reflexes, thus enlivening the whole.

864

All kinds of *camayeu*,[1] or colour on similar colour, end in the introduction either of a complemental contrast, or some variety of hue. Thus, Polidoro[2] in his black and white frescoes sometimes introduced a yellow vase, or something of the kind.

865

In general it may be observed that men have at all times instinctively striven after colour in the practice of the art. We need only observe daily, how soon amateurs proceed from colourless to coloured materials. Paolo Uccello painted coloured landscapes to colourless figures.

866

Even the sculpture of the ancients could not be exempt from the influence of this propensity. The Egyptians painted their bas-reliefs; statues had eyes of coloured stones. Porphyry draperies were added to marble heads and extremities, and variegated stalactites were used for the pedestals of busts. The Jesuits did not fail to compose the statue of their S. Luigi, in Rome, in this manner, and the most modern sculpture distinguishes the flesh from the drapery by staining the latter.

Editor's Notes

1 Or *Camaieu*, a painterly technique by which an image is executed either entirely in shades or tints of a single color or several hues unnatural to the object represented.

2 Polidoro da Caravaggio (about 1499–1543) a painter from Lombardy famed for his monochrome paintings on palace façades.

From: Johann Wolfgang von Goethe, *Theory of Colours*, 1820, translated from the German with notes by Charles Lock Eastlake (London: John Murray, 1840), 331–335.

3

"Of Turnerian Light"

John Ruskin

20. Of the three advantages possessed by the colourists over the chiaroscurists, the first is, that they have in the greater portions of their pictures *absolute* truth, [. . .] while the chiaroscurists have no absolute truth anywhere. With the colourists the shadows are right; the lights untrue: but with the chiaroscurists lights and shadows are both untrue. The second advantage is, that also the *relations* of colour are broader and vaster with the colourists from the chiaroscurists. Take, for example, that piece of drapery studied by Leonardo, in the Louvre, with white lights and black shadows.[1] Ask yourself, first, whether the real drapery was black or white. If white, then its high lights are rightly white; but its folds being black, it could not *as a mass* be distinguished from the black or dark objects in its neighbourhood. But the fact is, that a white cloth or handkerchief always *is* distinguished in daylight, as a *whole white thing*, from all that is coloured about it: we see at once that there is a white piece of stuff, and a red, or green, or grey one near it, as the case may be: and this relation of the white object to other objects *not* white, Leonardo has wholly deprived

himself of the power of expressing; while if the cloth were black or dark, much more has he erred by making its lights white. In either case, he has missed the large relation of mass to mass, for the sake of the small one of fold to fold. And this is more or less the case with all chiaroscurists; with all painters, that is to say, who endeavour in their studies of objects to get rid of the idea of colour, and give abstract shade. They invariably exaggerate the shadows, not with respect to the thing itself, but with respect to all around it; and they exaggerate the lights also, by leaving pure white for the high light of what in reality is grey, rose-coloured, or, in some way, not white.

21. This method of study, being peculiarly characteristic of the Roman and Florentine schools, and associated with very accurate knowledge of form and expression, has gradually got to be thought by a large body of artists the *grand* way of study; an idea which has been fostered all the more because it was an unnatural way, and therefore thought to be a philosophical one. Almost the first idea of a child, or a simple person looking at any thing, is, that it is a red, or a black, or a green, or a white thing. Nay, say the artists; that is an unphilosophical and barbarous view of the matter. Red and white are mere vulgar appearances; look no farther into the matter, and you will see such and such wonderful other appearances. Abstract those, *they* are the heroic, epic, historic, and generally eligible appearances. And acting on this grand principle, they draw flesh white, leaves white, ground white, everything white in the light, and everything black in the shade – and think themselves wise. But, the longer I live, the more ground I see to hold in high honour a certain sort of childishness or innocent susceptibility. Generally speaking, I find that when we first look at a subject, we get a glimpse of some of the greatest truths about it: as we

look longer, our vanity, and false reasoning, and half-knowledge, lead us into various wrong opinions; but as we look longer still, we gradually return to our first impressions, only with a full understanding of their mystical and innermost reasons; and of much beyond and beside them, not then known to us, now added (partly as a foundation, partly as a corollary) to what at first we felt or saw. It is thus eminently in this matter of colour. Lay your hand over the page of this book, – any child or simple person looking at the hand and book, would perceive, as the main fact of the matter, that a brownish pink thing was laid over a white one. The grand artist comes and tells you that your hand is not pink, and your paper is not white. He shades your fingers and shades your book, and makes you see all manner of starting veins, and projecting muscles, and black hollows, where before you saw nothing but paper and fingers. But go a little farther, and you will get more innocent again; you will find that, when "science has done its worst, two and two still make four;" and that the main and most important facts about your hand, so seen, are, after all, that it has four fingers and a thumb – showing as brownish pink things on white paper.

22. I have also been more and more convinced, the more I think of it, that in general *pride is at the bottom* of all great mistakes. All the other passions do occasional good, but whenever pride puts in *its* word, everything goes wrong, and what it might really be desirable to do, quietly and innocently, it is mortally dangerous to do, proudly. Thus, while it is very often good for the artist to make *studies* of things, for the sake of knowing their forms, with their high lights all white, the moment he does this in a haughty way, and thinks himself drawing in the great style, because he leaves high lights white, it is all over with

him; and half the degradation of art in modern times has been owing to endeavours, much fostered by the metaphysical Germans, to see things without colour, as if colour were a vulgar thing, the result being, in most students that they end by not being able to see anything at all; whereas the true and perfect way of studying any object is simply to look what its colour is in high light, and put that safely down, if possible; or, if you are making a chiaroscuro study, to take the grey answering to that colour, and cover the *whole* object at once with that grey, firmly resolving that no part of it shall be brighter than that; then look for the darkest part of it, and if, as is probable, its darkest part be still a great deal lighter than black, or than other things about it, assume a given shade, as dark as, with due reference to other things, you can have it, but no darker. Mark that for your extreme dark on the object, and between those limits get as much drawing as you can, by subtlety of gradation. That will tax your powers of drawing indeed; and you will find this, which seems a childish and simple way of going to work, requires verily a thousandfold more power to carry out than all the pseudo-scientific abstractions that ever were invented.

23. Nor can it long be doubted that it is also the most impressive way to others; for the third great advantage possessed by the colourists is, that the delightfulness of their picture, its sacredness, and general nobleness, are increased exactly in proportion to the quantity of light and of lovely colour they can introduce in *the shadows*, as opposed to the black and grey of chiaroscurists. I have already, in the *Stones of Venice*, Vol. II, Chap. V, 30–36, insisted upon the fact of the sacredness of colour, and its necessary connection with all pure and noble feeling. What we have seen of the use of colour by the poets will help to

confirm this truth; but perhaps I have not yet enough insisted on the simplest and readiest to hand of all proofs, – the way, namely, in which God has employed colour in His creation as the unvarying accompaniment of all that is purest, most innocent, and most precious; while for things precious only in material uses, or dangerous, common colours are reserved. Consider for a little while what sort of a world it would be if all flowers were grey, all leaves black, and the sky *brown*. Imagine that, as completely as may be, and consider whether you would think the world any whit more sacred for being thus transfigured into the hues of the shadows of Raphael's Transfiguration. Then observe how constantly innocent things are in bright colour; look at a dove's neck, and compare it with the grey back of a viper; I have often heard talk of brilliantly coloured serpents; and I suppose there are such – as there are gay poisons, like the foxglove and kalmia – types of deceit: but all the venomous serpents I have really *seen* are grey, brick-red, or brown, variously mottled; and the most awful serpent I have seen, the Egyptian asp, is precisely of the colour of gravel, or only a little greyer. So, again, the crocodile and alligator are grey, but the innocent lizard green and beautiful. I do not mean that the rule is invariable, otherwise it would be more convincing than the lessons of the natural universe are intended ever to be; there are beautiful colours on the leopard and tiger, and in the berries of the nightshade; and there is nothing very notable in brilliancy of colour either in sheep or cattle (though, by the way, the velvet of a brown bull's hide in the sun, or the tawny white of the Italian oxen, is, to my mind, lovelier than any leopard's or tiger's skin): but take a wider view of nature, and compare generally rainbows, sunrises, roses, violets, butterflies, birds, goldfish, rubies, opals, and corals, with alligators, hippopotami, lions, wolves, bears, swine, sharks, slugs, bones, fungi,[1] frogs, and corrupting, stinging, destroying things in general, and you will feel then how the question stands between the colourists and chiaroscurists, – which of them have nature and life on their side, and which have sin and death.

Author's Note

1 It is notable, however, that nearly all the poisonous agarics are scarlet or speckled, and wholesome ones brown or grey, as if to show us that things rising out of the darkness and decay are always most deadly when they are well drest.

From: John Ruskin, "Of Turnerian Light," *Modern Painters* IV, 1856, *The Complete Works* (Library Edition), ed. E.T. Cook and Alexander Wedderburn (London: George Allen, 1903–1912), 39 vols, vol. VI, 64–69.

4

French Discovery – Pencil of Nature

Who has not admired the splendid and wonderful representations in the camera obscura? – images so clear, so full of life, so perfectly representing every object in nature. These living pictures, by traversing the lens and mirrors, are thrown down with double beauty on the table of the camera obscura, by the radiant finger of light. The new art has been discovered to fix these wonderful images, which have hitherto passed away volatile – evanescent as a dream – to stop them at our will, on a substance finely sensible to the immediate action of light, and render them permanent before our eyes, in traces represented by tints in perfect harmony on each point, with different degrees of intensity.

We must not, however, believe, as has been erroneously reported to the public, with respect to these [Parisian] experiments, that the proper colours of objects are represented, in these images, by colours – they are only represented, with extreme truth by light, and every gradation of shade; – as an oil-painting is given by a perfect engraving, consisting of black lines; or perhaps, more akin to a design made with mathematical accuracy, and in acqua tinta; for there are no crossings of lines in the designs by the pencil of nature. Red, blue, yellow, and *green* &c., are rendered by combinations of light and shade; by demi-tints, more or less clear or obscure, according to the quantity of light in each colour. But in these copies, the delicacy of the design – the purity of the forms – the truth and harmony of tone – the aerial perspective – the high finish of the details, are all expressed with the highest perfection. The formidable lens, which often betrays monstrosities in the most delicate and aerial of our master-pieces, may here search for defects in vain. The creations of nature triumph. Far from betraying any defect, the highest magnifier only tends to shew more clearly its vast superiority. At each step, we find new objects to admire, revealing to us the existence of exquisite details, which escape the naked eye, even in reality. Nor can this astonish us when the radiant light, which can only act according to the immutable laws of nature, substitutes its rays for the hesitating pencil of the artist.

M. Daguerre has represented, from the Pont des Arts, and in a very small space, the whole of the magnificent buildings on the right bank of the Seine, including that part of the Louvre containing the grand gallery of pictures. Each line, each point, is rendered with a perfection quite unattainable by all means hitherto used. He has also reproduced the dark mass of Nôtre Dame, with its immense draperies and Gothic sculptures. He has also taken the view of a building, in the morning at eight o'clock, at mid-day, and at four o'clock in the afternoon, during rain, and in sunshine. Eight or ten minutes at most, in the climate of Paris, is sufficient; but, under a more ardent sun, such as that of Egypt, one minute will suffice. To artists and *savans* who travel, and who often find it impossible to prolong their stay at interesting places, this process must be most welcome.

The French journals, and reports of proceedings, however, admit that these admirable representations still leave something to be desired as to effect, when regarded as works of art. It is singular, they observe, that the power which created them seems to have abandoned them; and that *these works of light want light*. Even in those parts the most lighted, there is an absence of vivacity and effect; and it is allowed, that amidst all the harmony of their forms, these views appear subjected to the sober and heavy tone of colour imparted by a dull northern sky. It would appear, that by passing through the glasses of the optical arrangement of M. Daguerre, all the views are uniformly clothed with a melancholy aspect, like that given to the horizon by the approach of evening. Motion, it is obvious, can never be copied; and the attempt to represent animals and shoeblacks in action, consequently failed. Statuary is said to have been well-defined; but, hitherto, M. Daguerre has not succeeded in copying the living physiognomy in a satisfactory manner, though he does not despair of success.

It could not have escaped chemists, that various chemical products are sensibly affected by light. Some gases may remain together in the dark, without any effect, but a ray of light will cause instant explosion. Other bodies, such as the chloruret[1] of silver, are modified in colour. It at first takes a violet tint, afterwards becomes black. This property would, doubtless, have suggested the idea of applying it to the art of design. But, by this method, the most brilliant parts of the object become discoloured, and the darker parts remain white: this produces an effect contrary to the fact. And again, the continued action of the light tends to render the whole dark. Mr. Talbot's method would seem to be based on the use of the salts of silver with the addition of some substance, or covering, to prevent the further action of light, after the design was complete.

This discovery will doubtless make a great revolution in the arts of design; and, in a multitude of cases, will supersede old methods altogether inferior. The temporary interest of many may, at first, be affected; but whatever has the true character of good, cannot essentially do mischief. The invention of printing soon gave employment to many more than were employed as copyists. Even in our own time, the substitution of steel-plates for engraving, instead of copper, although fifty times as many copies may be taken from them, has, by the substitution of good engravings for indifferent ones, so extended the demand, that more steel-plates are now required than were formerly used of copper.

Editor's Note

1 Chloride.

From: "French Discovery – Pencil of Nature," from "The New Art," *The Literary Gazette: A Weekly Journal of Literature, Science, and the Finer Arts*, February 2, 1839, issue 1150, 74.

5

"The Progress and Present State of the Daguerreotype Art"

M. Claudet

Although the daguerreotype has hardly been in existence four years, it already ranks as one of the most prominent inventions of the present day, leaving scarcely any thing to look for in the way of improvement. It is true that it remains to find the means of reproducing the natural colours of objects; but, although there seems no dream too marvellous in the progress of discovery, still the idea of fixing the colours of the object in the camera obscura is so little in accordance with the present state of science and with the properties of the known elements, that we must be satisfied with the process as it is.

From: M. Claudet, No. VIII. "THE PROGRESS AND PRESENT STATE OF THE DAGUERREOTYPE ART," *Transactions of the Society, Instituted at London, for the Encouragement of Arts, Manufactures, and Commerce*, Vol. 55 (1843–1844), 89–110, 110.

6

"Calotypes"

Having so frequently and fully described the process of photography as discovered and practised by Mr. Fox Talbot, we now recur to the subject merely to notice the progress made in the art of portraiture, under the gentlemen's patent, by Mr. Collen.[1] The calotypes have the advantage, over the daguerreotypes, of hue and natural position. The tint is warm and by no means unpleasing; it resembles somewhat that of a proof on India paper, though more of a bistre colour; and the relation of feature is true to the beholder. The calotype portrait is not the first effect, as in the daguerreotype, wherein the face is changed from right to left and from left to right; but a secondary production, the reverse of the primary copy, correcting the error, reflecting a reflection. The result of the camera-process on the prepared paper is a black imperfect smudge, scarcely shewing the slightest resemblance to the sitter, and possessing a faint outline of form or feature. But this darkened skeleton, pressed down on other metal-washed paper by a plate of glass, permitting and stopping here and there the passage of the solar rays, is filled out to a full and faithful portrait on the surface of the receiving calotype. The likenesses are for the most part very correct, and comparatively of an extremely pleasing character.

Editor's Note

1 Henry Collen (1798–1879) trained as a miniaturist and during August 1841 obtained a license from Fox Talbot to operate the calotype process.

"Calotypes," *The Literary Gazette* (March 12, 1842), Issue 1312, 184.

7

"Colour in its Relation to Photography"

Charles Martel

The colour generally preferred by English photographers for their productions is stigmatized by eminent foreign critics as cold, unnatural, and monotonous. The particular hues to which we have given the preference may be simply a matter of taste or fancy, yet sufficiently marked to characterise the English school of photography, and, consequently, to become elevated into a national characteristic. Be that as it may, of this we may be certain, that in a miscellaneous exhibition of photographs, the productions of artists of various nations – as in the recent Architectural Photographic Society's Exhibition – it is quite an easy task to pick out the productions of English photographers by their peculiarities of colour, apart from other characteristics.

It cannot but be worth while to consider in what, in the eyes of continental photographers, our defects of colour consist. By comparison with their productions, it would appear to lie in our general preference for cold, purple hues, in which all subjects –

portrait, landscape, and architecture – are indiscriminately clothed. Our continental neighbours, on the contrary, give a marked preference to warm hues, as sepia, umber, bistre, &c.

In the exhibition referred to, our national peculiarities in colour were very marked, and a very useful lesson might have been learned there by those disposed to study it. Not only was an inferiority in colouring observable, but there were other features which perhaps it would not be flattering or pleasing to the vanity of many of our brother artists to particularise. The same mannerism, however, exists in another department of art – in engraving. It is just as easy to recognize an engraving by an English artist amid a crowd of others by foreign artists. There are epochs of style and manner in the history of Art. The present appears to be characterised by the mechanical. In engraving, the mechanical style was educed and fostered by the Annuals; they created a demand for works, to produce which an adequate amount of talent was not forthcoming, therefore its place had to be supplied by mechanical agencies and appliances.

[...]

The peculiarity of colour in photographs abides with the English artist, to whatever clime he may betake himself. Twenty years' residence in a foreign country does not deprive him of his idiosyncrasy, and whether his productions come from India, Australia, Turkey, or the Pyrenees, the inimitable British seal is impressed upon them.

From: Charles Martel, "Colour in its Relation to Photography," *The Photographic News*, Vol. IV, No. 102, August 17, 1860, 181–182, 181.

SECTION 2

"EXPOSED TO THE SUNBEAMS": CHEMICAL REACTIONS/ "VEGETABLE COLOURS"

8

An Essay on Combustion

Elizabeth Fulhame

Preface: iii–xii.

The possibility of making cloths of gold, silver, and other metals by chymical processes, occurred to me in the year 1780: the project being mentioned to Doctor Fulhame and some friends, was deemed improbable. However, after some time, I had the satisfaction of realizing the idea, in some degree, by experiment.

Animated by this small success, I have, from time to time, ever since, prosecuted the subject as far as pecuniary circumstances would permit.

I imagined in the beginning, that a few experiments would determine the problem; but experience soon convinced me, that a very great number indeed were necessary, before such an art could be brought to any tolerable degree of perfection.

A narration of the numerous experiments, which I made with this view, would far exceed the bounds I prescribe myself in this essay; I shall therefore present the reader only with a few, selecting such as I judge most interesting, and best adapted to illustrate the subject.

Though I was, after some considerable time, able to make small bits of cloth of gold, and silver, yet I did not think them worthy of public attention; but by persevering, I at length succeeded in making pieces of gold cloth, as large as my finances would admit.

Some time after this period, I found the invention was applicable to painting, and would also contribute to facilitate the study of geography: for I have applied it to some maps, the rivers of which I represented in silver, and the cities in gold. The rivers appearing, as it were, in silver streams, have a most pleasing effect on the sight, and relieve the eye of that painful search for the course, and origin, of rivers, the minutest branches of which can be splendidly represented in this way.

Notwithstanding this further success, I was dubious about the propriety of publishing this essay; I therefore shewed some specimens of these metallic stuffs to persons, whom I thought qualified to judge of them: some approved of them very much, and were pleased to say, that the invention would make an era in the arts; others thought it a pretty conceit; and others were of opinion, that the stuffs had not that splendour or burnished appearance, which could entitle them to public notice.

The latter opinion had much weight with me; for it must be allowed, that the specimens, which I shewed them, had not that lustre and polish necessary for shoulder-knots, lace, spangles, gold muslins, &c.; that some of them had a reddish cast, bordering on the colour of copper, some a purple, mixed with gold; and that some of them were unequal in the die, and seemed stained; which imperfections were owing to a partial reduction of the metal in the fibres of the silk.

But all these imperfections, except the want of that burnished lustre so necessary for gold lace, spangles, &c. I knew I could remedy; and therefore the criticism, as far it relates to them, had no great influence with me.

I am in possession of some pieces, one of which is about a yard in length, which have scarce any of these imperfections.

Moreover, that high polish of burnished gold, so necessary in spangles, lace, &c, would, in my opinion, be a great imperfection in gold stuffs designed for whole suits; as a person in such a habit, would look like a gilded statue.

I saw a piece of gold stuff made for the late King of Spain, which was of a purple colour, with gold wire shining through it, though rather obscurely; and it was much admired: I was so struck with its beauty, that I attempted to imitate it on a small bit of white silk; and succeeded, having produced a beautiful purple colour, with gold beaming through it.

Therefore, the want of that burnished appearance is no objection to this art; for the paler and cooler, to a certain degree, the colour of the gold is, the more lovely do these metallic cloths appear.

I made small bits of gold tiffany, which looked exceedingly beautiful; the fineness of the thread contributing much to that effect; and, in my opinion, such webs are inimitable by mechanical means.

Beside, though I am not able to make cloths like burnished gold, others of greater means and abilities may; for we cannot pretend to prescribe any limits to the perfection, at which chymistry, and the arts, may arrive.

However, I must acknowledge, that this unfavourable judgment suspended my intention of publishing this little work, until a celebrated philosopher happening, some time in October 1793, to see some of the same pieces, and indeed, some of the worst, viewed the performance in a very different light.

This illustrious friend of science, not only approved of the specimens shewn him, but offered to have a memoir on the subject presented to the Royal Society: but different incidents dissuaded me from that mode of publication, and induced me to adopt the present.

I now no longer hesitated about the propriety of publishing; for, every thing considered, I judged, that though this art could never be established, which is by no means my opinion, yet the experiments themselves, upon which I attempted to found it, as they are new, and seem to throw some light on the theory of combustion, are not unworthy the attention of Chymists.

Those who viewed my performance with a favourable eye, were of opinion, that I should dedicate this Essay to some patron of the arts; or apply for his Majesty's Royal letters patent, in order to reimburse the expense necessarily incurred in this investigation, an expense so disproportionate to the fortune which supported it, that nothing but a certain fatality, and the hope of reward, could induce me to persevere.

As to patrons, I have heard of such beings on the record of fame; but never saw one: on the contrary, it has been my lot to know of many, whose malignant breath, as far as its deadly influence can extend, never ceases to blast the unsheltered blossoms of science. – And as for a patent, had I even the means, I should perhaps never attempt it; for if we may judge of the future by the past, I can safely affirm, that such an application would be vain.

Thus circumstanced, I publish this Essay in its present imperfect state, in order to prevent the furacious attempts of the prowling plagiary, and the insidious pretender to chymistry, from arrogating to themselves, and assuming my invention, in plundering silence: for there are those, who, if they cannot by chymical, never fail by stratagem, and mechanical means, to deprive industry of the fruits, and fame, of her labours.

But the British empire should not forget, that she owes her power and greatness to commerce; that she is, as it were, the hive of the arts, and should not, by the sulphureous vapour of oppression, and neglect, compel her bees to swarm for protection to foreign climes, but rather permit them to roam in their native soil, and allow them, in the winter of life, to sip a little of the honey of their own industry.

The nation, whose evil genius withholds this protection, only sounds the trumpet of emigration; and must ere long lament her cities deserted, her fields brown with desolation, and herself the easy prey, and vile drudge of surrounding greatness.

I first imagined, that the proper title of this performance, should be, An Essay on the Art of making Cloths of Gold, Silver, and other Metals, by chymical processes; but reflecting on the imperfect state of the art, and that my experiments related not only to the reduction, but also to the calcination of metals, and other combustible bodies, I determined to entitle it, An Essay on Combustion, with a view to a new Art of Dying and Painting, which includes every thing the experiments can extend to.

As to the style, I have endeavoured to relate the experiments in a plain and simple manner, aiming more at perspicuity, than elegance.

I have adopted the French Nomenclature, as the terms of it are so framed, as to prevent circumlocution, assist the memory, by pointing out the combination, and state of the elements existing in each compound, as far they are known; advantages to be found in no other Nomenclature.

However, the English reader must regret, that the French chymists have not preferred the terms *air*, and *ammonia*, to the less harmonious sounds, *gas*, and *ammoniac*. I took the liberty of writing the latter *ammonia*.

I have not related my experiments in the order, in which they were made, sensible that such a narration would be tedious, and that a short extract from them would answer every purpose at present intended.

The experiments related I have endeavoured to arrange in such a manner, as mutually to illustrate each other, by contrasting the successful with those, that failed, thus pointing out a general principle, which forms a chain through the whole, connects all the experiments, shows their points of coincidence, and disagreement, and by this means furnishes us with *data*, by which, I hope, the art may be improved.

This arrangement also facilitates the perusal, and relieves the mind of that fatiguing attention, which must necessarily be given to an indigested mass of insulated experiments, that have no clue to connect them, but has, on the other hand, its disadvantages; for it throws a sameness on the work, incompatible with that variety which is often so agreeable.

My apparatus consisted chiefly of a few glass vessels for the solution of metals, and the formation of such elastic fluids, as I used. The cheapest, and the most simple of those described by Dr. Priestley answered my purpose.

Dr. Nooth's machine for combining carbonic acid with water, is very convenient for making small experiments with some kinds of gas; as the base of that machine serves to contain the materials, from which the gas is obtained; and the middle glass the cloth previously dipped in the metallic solution, on which the experiment is to be made.

The cloth may be suspended in this part of the machine, by means of a thread, and a cork.

As this machine is useful only in experiments on a very small scale, I sometimes used tall glass cylinders, in which I suspended the subject of the experiment, by means of a thread, a cork, and a bit of cement.

This cylinder I placed over a vessel containing the materials, which produced the gas.

It is very convenient to have cylinders of different sizes, proportioned to the scale, on which the experiments are to be made.

But machinery for confining elastic fluids is not always necessary; as most of the experiments may be performed in the open air.

It may appear presuming to *some*, that I should engage in pursuits of this nature, but averse from indolence, and having much leisure, my mind led me to this mode of amusement, which I found entertaining, and will I hope, be thought inoffensive by the liberal, and the learned. But censure is perhaps inevitable; for some are so ignorant, that they grow sullen and silent, and are chilled with horror at the sight of any thing, that bears the semblance of learning, in whatever shape it may appear; and should the *spectre* appear in the shape of *woman*, the pangs, which they suffer, are truly dismal.

There are others, who suffer the same torture in a still higher degree; but by virtue of an *old inspiring tripod*, on which ignorance, servility, or chance, has placed them, assume a dictatorship in science, and fancying their rights and prerogatives invaded, swell with rage, and are suddenly seized with a violent and irresistible desire of revenge, manifesting itself by innuendos, nods, whispers, sneers, grins, grimace, satanic smiles, and witticisms uttered sometimes in the acute, and sometimes in the nasal obtuse twang, with an affected hauteur, and contempt of the *spectre*; shrugs, and a variety of other contortions attending.

Sometimes the goblin, which thus agitates them, lurks latent, and nothing is perceived but hollow murmurs, portending storms: sometimes the lurking fiend darts with sidelong fury at the devoted object, which, if unarmed, falls a victim to the grisly monster.

But happily for human kind, the *magic tripod* drags none into its dizzy vortex, but those who are radically stupid, and malicious, who are the beasts of prey destined to hunt down unprotected genius, to stain the page of biography, or to rot unnoted in the grave of oblivion.

Although the surge of deliberate malice be unavoidable, its force is often spent in froth, and bubbles; for this little bark of mine has weathered out full many a storm, and stemmed the boisterous tide; and though the cargo be not rich, the dangers, which may hereafter be pourtrayed on *votive tablet*, may serve as a beacon to future mariners.

But happen what may, I hope I shall never experience such desertion of mind, as not to hold the helm with becoming fortitude against the storm raised by ignorance, petulant arrogance, and privileged dulness.

However, were I not encouraged by the judgment of some friends, and possessed of specimens, to shew the progress made in the art, I should never perhaps venture to publish this Essay; as I am sensible, it labours under many imperfections, which inaccuracy of observation, and the drapery of imagination, must spread over the whole; imperfections perhaps unavoidable in such a discussion.

Finding, the experiments could not be explained on any theory hitherto advanced, I was led to form an opinion different from that of M. Lavoisier, and other great names. Persuaded that we are not to be deterred from the investigation of truth by any authority however great, and that every opinion must stand or fall by its own merits, I venture with diffidence to offer mine to the world, willing to relinquish it, as soon as a more rational appears.

November 5th, 1794.

From: CHAPTER VIII. 'REDUCTION OF METALS BY LIGHT', 142–154.

[...]

EXP. 3. GOLD.

On the 24th of July a piece of silk was immersed in a solution of nitro-muriate of gold in water, and dried by a gentle heat; it was then suspended in a window, exposed to the sunbeams as much as possible: no change was perceived on it, till the 26th, when the margin of the silk began to assume a purple tinge, which increased gradually, and on the 29th exhibited a few obscure specks of reduced gold on the side of the silk opposed to the light.

The purple tinge continued to increase, and the yellow, which the solution of gold gave the silk, decreased gradually, till on the 27th of August the colour was a mixture of purple, and light brown.

The reduction of the gold seemed to keep pace with these changes of colour, and was very evident on some parts of the silk even in the gray light; but much more so in sunshine: these changes were observed till the 20th of October; the experiment was then discontinued; and scarce any reduced gold could be seen on the side of the silk not opposed to the light.

That this slight reduction of the gold, and changes of colour in the silk, depended on water absorbed from the air of the chamber, will appear from the following experiments.

EXP. 4. GOLD.

A bit of silk, which was dipped in the solution of gold employed in the preceding experiment, was dried, and suspended in a chrystal phial over dry carbonate of potash: the phial was then corked, and further secured from external humidity by covering the cork with wax: it was now placed in a dark closet 24 hours, that the carbonate of potash might have sufficient time to attract all the moisture, it could, from the air of the phial, before exposing it to the action of light.

The phial was then placed in a window, exposed, as much as possible, to the solar light, from the 24th of July to the 20th of October, and carefully observed: the same side of the silk was always opposed to the light, and had the yellow tinge, which the solution of gold gave, altered to a brownish yellow: but the other side of the silk suffered no visible change whatever; nor could any purple tint, or the smallest vestige of reduced gold be perceived.

Another bit of silk, which was immersed in the same solution of gold, and dried by a gentle heat, was suspended over some dry carbonate of potash, contained in a chrystal phial covered with black silk, and placed in a dark closet, during the same space of time, but underwent no visible change whatever.

Both these bits of silk were now taken out of the phials, and the gold was instantly restored to its metallic splendour by means of water and a solution of phosphorus in ether: a proof that the nitro-muriate of gold, in these bits of silk, suffered no change, during that space of time.

EXP. 5. GOLD.

A piece of silk, which was dipped in the same solution of gold, and placed on a china plate exposed to the sunbeams, was kept moderately wet with water during the experiment: the first alteration observed was, that the yellow colour of the silk began to change to a faint green, succeeded by a purple tinge, which in about fifteen minutes exhibited some particles of reduced gold: soon after the threads of the silk, which acquired this purple tint, were gilded with gold; and, in about an hour, the whole of the silk was covered with a superb coat of reduced gold, exhibiting the texture of the silk in a beautiful manner.

The purple tinge, which attended the reduction verged in some parts on red, and in others on blue.

This experiment, which is very amusing, I have repeated times unnumbered: and when the sun is powerful, and the solution of gold properly prepared, and of due strength, the coat of reduced gold is so bright, and dazzling, as to distress the eye of the beholder.

I find that the best way of preparing a solution of gold for this purpose is to separate the oxid of gold from its solution in nitro-muriatic acid by means of good ether.

The silk may be dipped in this solution, and when the ether evaporates, kept moderately wet with distilled water.

It was with this solution in ether that I first reduced gold in the fibres of silk, and it was by means of the same, I discovered, that water was a necessary condition in these reductions by light.

[...]

EXP. 9. SILVER.

A piece of silk was dipped in a solution of fused nitrate of silver in alcohol, and carefully dried: it was then suspended over a quantity of concentrated sulphuric acid in a chrystal phial, which was coated with a double fold of black paper, and gum arabic, reaching somewhat above the level of the acid, to prevent the light from acting on it: the phial was corked, and to exclude moisture more effectually, the cork was covered with wax.

The phial was now placed in a dark closet 24 hours, that the humidity of the enclosed silk and air might be attracted by the acid: it was then placed in a window, exposed as much as possible to the rays of the sun, from the 19th of July to the 26th of October: but the silk underwent no visible change whatever: its white colour remained pure, and unaltered.

The silk, at the end of this period, was taken out of the phial, and wetted with water: a solution of phosphorus in ether was then applied to it; and instantly the metallic splendour of the silver appeared.

Another bit of silk, which was immersed in a solution of nitrate of silver in water, and dried in the dark, was suspended over dry carbonate of potash in a phial, and placed in a dark closet about two months: the silk underwent no visible alteration whatever: its white colour remained pure.

I was desirous of knowing, if the nitrate of silver in this bit of silk suffered any change, that might render it incapable of reduction: I therefore took it out of the phial, and divided it into two parts: one of these was wetted with water, and the silver was instantly reduced by a solution of phosphorus in ether. The other part, which was suspended in a window, exposed to the air of the chamber, and rays of the sun, soon acquired a reddish brown colour.

Hence it is evident, that these changes of colour indicate partial reductions of the metal; and that they never happen without the presence of water.

[. . .]

The experiments detailed in this Chapter, prove beyond the power of contradiction,

1. That water is essential to the reduction of metals by light: for these experiments demonstrate, that the reduction cannot take place without water, and that it is always in proportion to the quantity of that fluid present.

2. That light does not reduce metals by giving them phlogiston, as Messrs. Macquer and Scheele supposed; for were this opinion true, light should reduce them without the aid of water, and as well with alcohol as with water.

3. Light does not reduce metals by fusing and expelling their oxygen, as the antiphlogistians imagine; for were this its mode of agency, the reduction should happen without the assistance of water, and as well with alcohol as with water.

4. Light is a combustible body; for it acts like hydrogen, phosphorus, sulphur, and charcoal, in the reduction of metals.

Since water then is essential to the reduction of metals by light, and since light does not reduce metals by giving them phlogiston, nor by fusing and expelling their oxygen, it follows, that the water is either decomposed, or that it unites with, metallic earths, and constitutes their phlogiston, or that it unites with, and separates their oxygenous principle: but as the two last suppositions are inadmissible, it is obvious that light reduces the metals by decomposing water.

From: Elizabeth Fulhame, *An Essay on Combustion, with a view to a New Art of Dying and Painting Wherein the Phlogistic and Antiphlogistic Hypotheses are Proved Erroneous* (London: printed for the Author by J. Cooper, 1794).

9

"An Account of a Method of Copying Paintings upon Glass"

Thomas Wedgwood and Humphry Davy

White paper, or white leather moistened with a solution of nitrate of silver, undergoes no change when kept in a dark place; but on being exposed to the day light it speedily changes colour, and after passing through different shades of grey and brown, becomes at length nearly black.

The alterations of colour take place more speedily in proportion as the light is more intense. In the direct beams of the sun, two or three minutes are sufficient to produce the full effect. In the shade, several hours are required, and light transmitted through different coloured glasses, acts upon it with different degrees of intensity. Thus, it is found, that red rays, or the common sunbeams passed through red glass, have very little action upon it: yellow and green are more efficacious; but blue and violet light produce the most decided and powerful effects.

The consideration of these facts enables us readily to understand the method by which the outlines and shades of paintings on glass may be copied, or profiles of figures procured, by the agency of light. When a white surface, covered with a solution of nitrate of silver, is placed behind a painting on glass exposed to the solar light; the rays transmitted through the differently painted surfaces produce distinct tints of brown or black, sensibly differing in intensity according to the shades of the picture, and where the light is unaltered, the colour of the nitrate becomes deepest.

When the shadow of any figure is thrown upon the prepared surface, the part concealed by it remains white, and the other parts speedily become dark.

For copying paintings on glass, the solution should be applied on leather; and, in this case, it is more readily acted upon than when paper is used.

After the colour has been once fixed upon the leather or paper, it cannot be removed by the application of water, or water and soap, and it is in a high degree permanent.

The copy of a painting, or the profile, immediately after being taken, must be kept in an obscure place. It may indeed be examined in the shade, but, in this case, the exposure should be only for a few minutes; by the light of candles or lamps, as commonly employed, it is not sensibly affected.

No attempts that have been made to prevent the uncoloured parts of the copy or profile, from being acted upon by light have as yet been successful. They have been covered with a thin coating of fine varnish, but this has not destroyed their susceptibility of becoming coloured; and even after repeated washings, sufficient of the active part of the saline matter will still adhere to the white parts of the leather or paper, to cause them to become dark when exposed to the rays of the sun.

Besides the applications of this method of copying that have just been mentioned, there are many others. And it will be useful for making delineations of all such objects as are possessed of a texture partly opaque and partly transparent. The woody fibres of leaves, and the wings of insects, may be pretty accurately represented by means of it, and in this case, it is only necessary to cause the direct solar light to pass through them, and to receive the shadows upon prepared leather.

When the solar rays are passed through a print and thrown upon prepared paper, the unshaded parts are slowly copied; but the lights transmitted by the shaded parts, are seldom so definite as to form a distinct resemblance of them by producing different intensities of colour.

The images formed by means of a camera obscura, have been found too faint to produce, in any moderate time, an effect upon the nitrate of silver. To copy these images, was the first object of Mr. Wedgwood, in his researches on the subject, and for this purpose he first used the nitrate of silver, which was mentioned to him by a friend, as a substance very sensible to the influence of light; but all his numerous experiments as to their primary end, proved unsuccessful.

In following these processes, I have found, that the images of small objects, produced by means of the solar microscope, may be copied without difficulty on prepared paper. This will probably be a useful application of the method; that it may be employed successfully however, it is necessary that the paper be placed at but a small distance from the lens.

With regard to the preparation of the solution, I have found the best proportions those of 1 part of nitrate to about 10 of water. In this case, the quantity of the salt applied to the leather or paper, will be sufficient to enable it to become tinged, without affecting its composition, or injuring its texture.

In comparing the effects produced by light upon muriate of silver, with those produced upon nitrate, it seemed evident, that the muriate was the most susceptible, and both were more readily acted upon when moist than when dry, a fact long known. Even in the twilight, the colour of moist muriate of silver spread upon paper, slowly changed from white to faint violet; though under similar circumstances no immediate alteration was produced upon the nitrate.

The nitrate, however, from its solubility in water, possesses an advantage over the muriate; though leather or paper may, without much difficulty, be impregnated with this last substance, either by diffusing it through water, and applying it in this form, or by immersing paper moistened with the solution of the nitrate in very diluted muriatic acid.

To those persons not acquainted with the properties of the salts containing oxide of silver, it may be useful to state, that they produce a stain of some permanence, even when momentarily applied to the skin, and in employing them for moistening paper or leather, it is necessary to use a pencil of hair, or a brush.

From the impossibility of removing by washing, the colouring matter of the salts from the parts of the surface of the copy, which have not been exposed to light; it is probable that both in the case of the nitrate and muriate of silver, a portion of the metallic oxide abandons its acid, to enter into union with the animal or vegetable substance, so as to form with it an insoluble compound. And, supposing that this happens, it is not improbable, but that substances may be found capable of destroying this compound either by simple or complicated affinities. Some experiments on this subject have been imagined, and an account of the results of them may possibly appear in a future number of the Journals. Nothing but a method of preventing the unshaded parts of the delineation from being coloured by exposure to the day is wanting, to render the process as useful as it is elegant.

"An Account of a Method of copying Paintings upon Glass, and of Making profiles by the Agency of Light Upon the Nitrate of Silver, Invented by T. Wedgwood, Esq. With Observations by H. Davy." *Journals of the Royal Institution of Great Britain*, 22 June 1802, Vol. 1, no. 9, 170–174.

10

"On the Action of the Rays of the Solar Spectrum on Vegetable Colours, and Some New Photographic Processes"

John F. W. Herschel

In photographic processes, where silver and other metals are used, the effect of light is so rapid that the state of the weather, as to gloom or sunshine, is of little moment. It is otherwise in the class of photographic actions now to be considered, in which exposure to the concentrated spectrum for many hours, to clear sunshine for several days, or to dispersed light for whole months, is requisite to bring on many of the effects described, and those some of the most curious. Moreover, in such experiments, when unduly prolonged by bad weather, the effects due to the action of light become mixed and confounded with those of spontaneous changes in the organic substances employed, arising from the influence of air, and especially of moisture, &c., and so give rise to contradictory conclusions, or at all events preclude definite results, and obscure the perception of characters which might serve as guides in an intricate inquiry, and afford hints for the conduct of future experiment. It is owing to these causes that I am unable to present the results at which I have arrived, in any sort of regular or systematic connection; nor should I have ventured to present them at all to the Royal Society, but in the hope that, desultory as they are, there may yet be found in them matter of sufficient interest to render their longer suppression unadvisable, and to induce others more favourably situated as to climate, to prosecute the subject.

[...]

Of the Colours of Flowers in general under the action of the Spectrum

163. In operating on the colours of flowers I have usually proceeded as follows:- the petals of the fresh flowers, or rather such parts of them as possessed a uniform tint, were crushed to a pulp in a marble mortar, either alone, or with the addition of alcohol, and the juice expressed by squeezing the pulp in a clean linen or cotton cloth. It was then spread on paper with a flat brush, and dried in the air without artificial heat, or at most with the gentle warmth which rises in the ascending current of air from an Arnott stove. If alcohol be not added, the application on paper must be performed immediately, since exposure

to the air of the juices of most flowers (in some cases even for a few minutes) irrecoverably changes or destroys their colour. If alcohol be present this change does not usually take place, or is much retarded; for which reason, as well as on account of certain facilities afforded by its admixture in procuring an even tint (to be presently stated), this addition was commonly, but not always made.

164. Most flowers give out their colouring matter readily enough, either to alcohol or water. Some, however, as the Escholzias and Calceolarias, refuse to do so, and require the addition of alkalies, others of acids, &c. When alcohol is added, it should, however, be observed that the tint is often, apparently, much enfeebled, or even discharged altogether, and that the tincture, when spread on paper, does not reappear of its due intensity till after complete drying. [. . .] And in all cases long keeping deteriorates the colours and alters the qualities of the alcoholic tinctures themselves, so that they should always be used as fresh as possible.

165. If papers tinged with vegetable colours are intended to be preserved, they must be kept perfectly dry and in darkness. A close tin vessel, the air of which is dried by quicklime (carefully enclosed in double paper bags, well pasted at the edges to prevent the dust escaping), is useful for this purpose. Moisture (as already mentioned, especially assisted by heat) destroys them for the most part rapidly, though some (as the colour of the *Senecio splendens*) resist obstinately. Their destructibility by this agency, however, seems to bear no distinct relation to their photographic properties.

166. This is also the place to observe that the colour of a flower is by no means always, or usually, that which its expressed juice imparts to white paper. In many cases the tints so imparted have no

resemblance to the original hue. Thus, to give only a few instances, the red damask rose of that intense variety of colour, commonly called by florists the Black Rose, gives a dark blue, as do also the clove carnation and the black holyoak; a fine dark brown variety of Sparaxis gave a dull olive green; and a beautiful rose-coloured tulip, a dirty bluish green; but perhaps the most striking case of this kind is that of a common sort of red poppy (*Papaver Rheum*?), whose expressed juice imparts a rich and most beautiful blue colour, whose elegant properties as a photographic material will be further alluded to hereafter.[1]

167. This change of colour is probably owing to different causes in different flowers. In some it undoubtedly arises from the escape of carbonic acid, but this as a general cause for the change from red to blue, has, I am aware, been controverted.[2] In some (as in the case with the yellow Ranunculi) it seems to arise from a chemical alteration depending on absorption of oxygen; and in others, especially where the expressed juice coagulates on standing, to a loss of vitality or disorganization of the molecules. The fresh petal of a single flower, merely crushed by rubbing on dry paper, and instantly dried, leaves a stain much more nearly approximating to the original hue. This, for example, is the only way in which the fine blue colour of the common field Veronica can be imparted to paper. Its expressed juice, however quickly prepared, when laid on with a brush, affords only a dirty neutral gray, and so of many others. But in this way no even tint can be had, which is a first requisite to the experiments now in question, as well as their application to photography.

168. To secure this desirable evenness of tint, the following manipulation will generally be found successful. The paper should be moistened at the back by sponging and blotting off. It should then be

pinned on a board, the moist side downwards, so that two of its edges (suppose the right-hand and lower ones) shall project a little beyond those of the board. The board then inclined twenty or thirty degrees to the horizon, the alcoholic tincture (mixed with a very little water, if the petals themselves be not very juicy) is to be applied with a brush in strokes from left to right, taking care *not to* go over the edges which rest on the board, but *to* pass clearly over those which project, and observing also to carry the tint from below upwards by quick sweeping strokes, leaving no dry spaces between them, but keeping up a continuity of wet surface. When all is wet, cross them by another set of strokes from above downwards, so managing the brush as to leave no floating liquid on the paper. It must then be dried as quickly as possible over a stove, or in a current of warm air, avoiding, however, such heat as may injure the tint. The presence of alcohol prevents the solution of the gummy principle, which, when present, gives a smeary surface; but the evenness of tint given by this process results chiefly from that singular intestine movement which always takes place when alcohol is in the act of separation from water by evaporation – a movement which disperses knots and blots in the film of liquid with great energy, and spreads them over the surrounding surface.

169. The action of the spectrum, or of white light, on the colours of flowers and leaves, is extremely various, both as regards its total intensity and the distribution of the active rays over the spectrum. But certain peculiarities in this species of action obtain almost universally.

1st. The action is *positive*, that is to say, light destroys colour; either totally, or leaving a residual tint, on which it has no further, or a very much slower action. And thus is effected a sort of chromatic analysis, in which two distinct elements of colour are separated, by destroying the one and leaving the other outstanding. The older the paper, or the tincture with which it is stained, the greater is the amount of this residual tint.

2nd. The action of the spectrum is confined, or nearly so, to the region of it occupied by the luminous rays, as contra-distinguished both from the so-called chemical rays, beyond the violet, which act with the chief energy on argentine compounds, but are here for the most part ineffective, on the one hand, and on the other, from the thermic rays beyond the red, which appear to be totally so. Indeed, I have hitherto observed no instance of the extension of this description of photographic action on vegetable colours beyond, or even *quite* up to the extreme red.

170. Besides these, it may also be observed that the rays effective in destroying a given tint, are, in a great many cases, those whose union produces a colour complementary to the tint destroyed, or at least one belonging to that class of colours to which such complementary tint may be referred. For example, yellows tending towards orange are destroyed with more energy by the blue rays; blues by the red, orange, and yellow rays; purples and pinks by yellow and green rays.

[. . .]

Colours of particular Flowers

[. . .]

177. *Common ten-weeks Stock, Mathiola annua.* – The colour imparted by the petals of the *double variety* of this flower[3] to alcohol (at least when spread on paper, for it is in great measure dormant

in liquid tincture) is a rich and florid rose-red, varying, however, from a fiery tint almost amounting to scarlet, on the one hand, to a somewhat crimson or slightly purplish red on the other, according to the accidents of its preparation, or the paper used. When fresh prepared it is considerably sensitive, an hour or two of exposure to sunshine being sufficient to produce a sensible discoloration, and two or three days entirely to whiten it. This quality is greatly deteriorated by keeping, but papers prepared with it even after eight or ten months, still with patience yield extremely beautiful photographs, several specimens of which in various states of the tincture are submitted for inspection to the meeting. Exposed to the spectrum, the rays chiefly active in operating the discoloration are found to be those extending from the yellow to the less refrangible red, beyond which rays the action terminates abruptly. Above the yellow it degrades rapidly to a minimum in the blue, beyond which it recovers somewhat, and attains a second but much feebler maximum in the violet rays.

178. Paper stained with the tincture of this flower is changed to a vivid scarlet by acids, and to green by alkalies; if ammonia be used the red colour is restored as the ammonia evaporates, proving the absence of any acid quality in the colouring matter sufficiently energetic to coerce the elastic force of the alkaline gas. Sulphurous acid whitens it, as do the alkaline sulphites; but this effect is transient, and the red colour is slowly restored by free exposure to air, especially with the aid of light, whose influence in this case is the more remarkable, being exactly the reverse of its ordinary action on this colouring principle, which it destroys irrecoverably, as above stated. The following experiments were made to trace and illustrate this curious change.

179. Two photographic copies of engravings taken on paper tinted with this colour were placed in a jar of sulphurous acid gas, by which they were completely whitened, and all traces of the pictures obliterated. They were then exposed to free air, the one in the dark, the other in the sunshine. Both recovered, but the former much more slowly than the latter. The restoration of the picture exposed to sun was completed in twenty-four hours, that in the dark not till after a lapse of two or three days.

Author's Notes

1 A semicultivated variety was used, having dark purple spots at the bases of the petals. The common red poppy of the chalk (*Papaver hybridum*) gives a purple colour much less sensitive and beautiful.

2 NICHOLSON'S Journal.

3 That imparted by the single flowers is very much less sensitive, as is also that of the dull red or purplish variety, whether double or single. The most florid red double flowers in the height of their flowering, yield the best colour.

From: "Sir John F. W. Herschel, On the Action of the Rays of the Solar Spectrum on Vegetable Colours, and Some New Photographic Processes," *Philosophical Transactions of the Royal Society of London*, Vol. 132 (1842), 181–214.

SECTION 3

"GRAPHY" AND "PHOTOS": THE COLOR PURPLE

11

PURPURA ANGLICANA, being a discovery of a shell-fish found on the shores of the Severn

W. Cole

There being many Natural things, which I have formerly, and of late, happily found in the South and West Parts of *England*, not as I can find published by any *Author*; besides many more which have been discovered by the industrious Exquisitions of diverse ingenious and curious Searches of Nature; (as also others which were thought to be Exotiques;) I have reason to believe, that there are many more (for incouragement of such inquirers) yet undiscovered in this our Native Country. Among others, that of the *Purple-Fish*, which I found the last Winter, on the Sea Coasts of *Somerset-shire*, and the shores of *South Wales* opposite to it; which also I doubt not but may be found on the other Coasts of *England*, especially the South and Western parts, (in which I am almost assured I have formerly seen them, tho' then unknown to me,) where there are Rocks and great Pebbles, and where the Tides run not too strong. Which Discovery I do not pretend to be so made by me, as having no hint of it before: For in *October*, 1684, there were two Ladies at *Mynehead*, where I then was, who seeing what Collections I had made of Natural things in those Parts, told me, there was a certain Person living by the Sea-side, in some Port or Creek in *Ireland*, who made considerable gain, by marking with a delicate durable Crimson Colour, fine Linnen of Ladies, Gent. & c. sent from many parts of that island, with their Names, or otherwise as they pleased; which they told me, (as they were informed,) was made by some liquid substance taken out of a *Shell-fish*; upon which I showed them all the Shells I had found on that Coast; one of them thought it to be taken out of a Limpet; the other out of that Shell here figured and described; but neither of them could inform me out of what part it was taken in either. After their departure from that Port, I made Experiments on all the *Shell-fishes*, in which I might probably think to find it; and brake them while the fishes were alive in them, and with a shore pointed Pencil of Horse hair (no other instrument being so convenient) I tried every part of each, which I imagined might yield the Colour; but upon washing the Linnen which I had marked, in scalding water, with soap, there appeared nothing of any colour upon them; upon which I was ready to give over any farther search, but at length trying that part, in which I least thought the Tincture lay, it immediately turned to a light green; which being presently dryed and washed, as before, there appeared that delicate colour they told me of, as aforesaid.

The whole process, upon my oft repeated Experiments, was as followeth.

These Shells, being harder than most of other kinds, are to be broken with a smart stroak of a hammer, on a plate of Iron, or firm piece of Timber, with their mouth downwards, so as not to crush the Body of the Fish within: The broken pieces being pickt off, there will appear a white Vein, lying transversly in a little furrow or cleft, next to the head of the Fish, which must be digg'd out with the stiff point of the Horse hair pencil, being made short and tapering; which must be so formed, by reason of the viscous clamminess of that white Liquor in the Vein, that so by its stiffness, it may drive in the Matter into the fine Linnen, or white Silk; which, altho' I have not yet tried it, will (I think) be better than on Linnen, and make the colour appear more bright and vivid by its reflection, since which I have tried it on white Sarsnet, and find it so.

The Letters, Figures, or what else shall be made on the Linnen or Silk (as much forced in, as it can be by the pencil) will presently appear as a pleasant *light green colour*; and if placed in the *Sun*, will change into the following colours; *i.e.* if in Winter, about noon, if in the Summer, an hour or two after Sun rising, and so much before setting, for in the heat of the day, in Summer, the colours will come on so fast, that the succession of each, will scarce be distinguished; next to the first *light green*, it will appear of a *deep green*; and in few minutes change into a full and very fair *Sea green*; after which in a few minutes more, it will alter into a *Watchet blue*; from that, in a little time more, it will be of a *Purplish red*: after which, lying about an hour or two, (supposing the *Sun* still shining,) it will be of a very *deep Purple red*, beyond which the *Sun* can do no more.

{*Note*, that these changes are made faster or slower, according to the degrees of the *Sun's* heat.

But then the last and most beautiful colour, (after washing in scalding water and soap) will (the Matter being again put out in the *Sun* or wind to dry) be much a differing colour from all those mention'd, i.e. of a fair bright *Crimson*, or near to the *Princes Colour*, which afterwards, notwithstanding there is no use of any Stiptic to bind the colour, will continue the same, if well ordered; as I have found in handkerchiefs, that have been washed more than 40 times; only it will be somewhat allayed from what it was after the first-washing. I made large Letters on so many cloaths, as there are distinct colours, to put them into a Book, which kept them from the *Air*; I have several months after, showed the various colours distinct, as aforesaid; yet by often opening the Book, and so exposing them to the *Air*, all the colours, excepting the two last (I mean before washing either) will fade, but all the colours, being washed, will be one and the same. While the Cloath so writ upon, lyes in the *Sun*, it will yield a very strong fetid smell; (which divers who have smelt it could not endure) as if *Garlick* & *Assa-fatida* were mixt together; which I proved but few days before I wrote this, tho' it had been at least twelve months, kept in a Book; which before it was laid in the *Sun*, had very little of that smell. I have farther observed, that the cloath dryed and washt soon after it is wrote on, will appear fresher and brighter, then after being kept in a Book; as I found by some I newly caused to be washt, after they had been 14 months so kept.

The Shells are of divers colours, but the most part of them white; some are red, when newly taken off the Rocks; some yellow; others of both those colours; some a blackish brown; many a Sandy colour; and some few striped with white and brown parallel lines: I have herewith sent you most of the colours, with one of the largest I have found, and one of the least, with several of the middle sized. *vid. the figures:* the *Operculum.*

The first linen Cloaths marked with Letters and Names, I sent to Dr. *Plot* in *Nov.* 1684, being then one of the *Secretaries to the Royal Society in London*, to whom he communicating my *Letter* containing my first *Observations*, and also shewing the Linnen so markt (at the same time) advised me that it was so acceptable to them, that they were pleased to order him to return me their thanks; and that they had appointed some Gent. to wait on His late *Majesty* with them; who (with diverse Persons of Honour to whom they were shown) was much pleased with the sight, and relation of the discovery, as new to him.

From: W. Cole, *PURPURA ANGLICANA, being a discovery of a Shell-Fish found on the Shores of the Severn, in which there is a vein containing a juice giving the delicate and durable Tincture of the Antient, rich, Tyrian PURPLE; of which it is an undoubted Species: The Knowledge of which, hath been lost for many Ages. With Experimental OBSERVATIONS upon it, and Figures of the Shells.* (London: Joseph Streater, 1689), 1–9, 1–4.

12

“The Action of Light on the Colouring Matter from the ‘Murex’”

The photogenic properties of the mollusk, from which the ancients are supposed to have obtained their famed Tyrean purple-dye, have some time since, been investigated by M. Lacaze Duthiers, who submitted a very elaborate memoir on this curious and interesting subject to the *Academie des Scienc*es. In the first place it is necessary to premise that the term *purple* has, at various periods in the world's history, been applied to various colours more or less red. Strictly speaking, it should be restricted to the pure secondary colour of the prismatic spectrum composed of pure red and pure blue, in which blue is in greater proportion than it is in violet, which may be considered as composed of equal quantities of pure prismatic blue and red.

[. . .]

The action of light develops the three primary colours in the following order:- yellow, blue, red. Between these we find green resulting from the mixture of yellow with blue, and violet resulting from mixture of blue with red. In making the experiment slowly – that is, in diffused light – the succession of colours may be distinctly observed. But while the yellow disappears when the action of light is prolonged, the blue always remains in notable quantity – so that the red is never found (naturally) alone, and the hue of the purple is always more or less violet.

These properties are placed beyond the reach of doubt by the possibility of producing photographs upon silk or woollen tissues; and the results obtained without exhibiting the perfection of ordinary photographs exhibit, nevertheless, good detail and vigorous tones.

In a photographic image thus obtained we recognise some of the colours mentioned above. The greenish yellow corresponds to white, and the violet, more or less deep, to the blacks of ordinary photographs.

From: "The Action of Light on the Colouring Matter from the 'Murex,'" *British Journal of Photography*, London, Vol. 7, Issue 125, September 1, 1860: 252–253.

13

“The Queen of the Air: Athena Keramitis II”

John Ruskin

91. [. . .] As far as I can trace the colour perception of the Greeks, I find it all founded primarily on the degree of connection between colour and light; the most important fact to them in the colour of red being its connection with fire and sunshine; so that “purple” is, in its original sense, “fire-colour,” and the scarlet, or orange of dawn, more than any other, fire-colour. I was long puzzled by Homer’s calling the sea purple; and misled into thinking he meant the colour of cloud shadows on green sea; whereas he really means the gleaming blaze of the waves under wide light. Aristotle’s idea (partly true) is that light, subdued by blackness, becomes red; and blackness heated or lighted, also becomes red. Thus, a colour may be called purple because it is light subdued (and so death is called “purple” or “shadowy” death); or else it may be called purple as being shade kindled with fire, and thus said of the lighted sea; or even of the sun itself, when it is thought of as a luminary opposed to the whiteness of the moon: “purpureos inter

soles, et candida lunæ sidera", or of golden hair: "pro purpureo pœnam solvens scelerata capillo"; while both ideas are modified by the influence of an earlier form of the word, which has nothing to do with fire at all, but only with mixing or staining; and then, to make the whole group of thoughts inextricably complex, yet rich and subtle in proportion to their intricacy, the various rose and crimson colours of the murex-dye, – the crimson and purple of the poppy, and fruit of the palm – and the association of all of these with the hue of blood;- partly direct, partly through a confusion between the word signifying "slaughter" and "palm-fruit colour," mingle themselves in, and renew the whole nature of the old word; so that, in later literature, it means a different colour, or emotion of colour, in almost every place where it occurs: and casts around for ever the reflection of all that has been dipped in its dyes.

92. So that the word is really a liquid prism, and stream of opal. And then, last of all, to keep the whole history of it in the fantastic course of a dream, warped here and there into wild grotesque, we moderns, who have preferred to rule over coal-mines instead of the sea (and so have turned the everlasting lamp of Athena into a Davy's safety-lamp in the hand of Britannia, and Athenian heavenly lightning into British subterranean "damp"), have actually got our purple out of coal instead of the sea! And thus, grotesquely, we have had enforced on us the doubt that held the old word between blackness and fire, and have completed the shadow, and the fear of it, by giving it a name from battle, "Magenta."

From: John Ruskin, "The Queen of the Air, II. Athena Keramitis," 1869, *The Complete Works of John Ruskin* (Library Edition) eds. E. T. Cook and Alexander Wedderburn (London: George Allen 1903–1912), 39 vols, Vol. XIX, 379–380.

SECTION 4

"APOLLO AND APELLES": COLORING BY HAND

14

"Artists Who Painted with the Pencil"

Pliny the Elder

[Apelles's] inventions, too, in the art of painting, have been highly serviceable to others; but one thing there was in which no one could imitate him. When his works were finished, he used to cover them with a black varnish, of such remarkable thinness, that while by the reflection it gave more vivacity to the colours, and preserved them from the contact of dust and dirt, its existence could only be detected by a person when close enough to touch it. In addition to this, there was also this other great advantage attending it: the brightness of the colours was softened thereby, and harmonized to the sight, looking as though they had been viewed from a distance, and through a medium of specular-stone; the contrivance, by some indescribable means, giving a sombreness to colours which would otherwise have been too florid.

[. . .]

At the same period flourished Protogenes, as already stated. He was a native of Caunus, a place held in subjection by the Rhodians. Great poverty in his early days, and extreme application to his art, were the causes of his comparative unproductiveness [. . .] Of all his compositions, however, the palm has been awarded to his Ialysus, now at Rome, consecrated in the Temple of Peace there. [. . .] In order to protect this picture against the effects of ill-usage and old age, he painted it over four times, so that when an upper coat might fail, there would be an under one to succeed it. There is in this picture the figure of a dog, which was completed in a very remarkable manner, inasmuch as accident had an equal share with design in the execution of it. The painter was of opinion that he had not given the proper expression to the foam at the mouth of the animal, panting for breath, as it was represented; while, with all other parts of the picture, a thing extremely difficult with him, he was perfectly satisfied. The thing that displeased him was, the evident traces of art in the execution of it, touches which did not admit of any diminution, and yet had all the appearance of being too laboured, the effect produced being far removed from his conception of the reality: the foam, in fact, bore the marks of being painted, and not of being the natural secretion of the animal's mouth. Vexed and tormented by this dilemma, it being his wish to depict truth itself, and not something that only bore a semblance of truth, he effaced it again and again, changed his pencil for another, and yet by no possibility could satisfy himself. At last, quite out of temper with an art, which, in spite of him, would still obtrude itself, he dashed his sponge against the vexatious spot; when behold: the sponge replaced the colours that it had just removed, exactly in accordance with his utmost wishes, and thus did chance represent Nature in a painting.

From: Pliny the Elder, "Artists Who Painted with the Pencil," *The Natural History*, Book 25, Ch. 36, trans. John Bostock and H. T. Riley (London: Taylor & Francis, 1855).

15

Letters Upon the Art of Miniature Painting

L. Mansion

LETTER V.

Mr. Deville to Miss Ellen

Paris, May 27th, 1821.

To comply with your wish of acquiring instruction, charming Ellen, I will in this letter immediately enter upon the subject that seems to interest you so much, and tell you that some persons, who only judge of the merit and difficulty of a picture by its size, pronounce, without hesitation, miniature-painting to be easier than any other. I am far from being of that opinion: on the contrary, I maintain that a miniature-painter, who wishes to arrive at perfection, has more difficulties to overcome than a painter in oil who confines himself to portrait-painting. The same knowledge of drawing and colouring is required for each, but the colours for miniature-painting being more difficult to use, certain effects are often produced at once in oil by one stroke of the pencil, which in miniature can be brought out only by care and labour. This will prove to you, dear Miss Ellen, how essential it is to be well-acquainted with what we undertake, so as not to employ colour indiscriminately in the hope of being favoured by Fortune, who so often laughs at the efforts of man! If a miniature-painter were to trust the success of his work to her, he would be nearly as mad as one, who, shaking together a great number of printing-letters, should hope, solely by that means, to become one day the author of a treatise upon philosophy or jurisprudence. With respect to us, we will follow a different method, directing our attention to become well acquainted with the necessary materials. We will make use of them at first with diffidence, and when by habit and experience we shall have acquired more confidence, we will not be afraid to work more boldly, without however losing sight of moderation. You will find in the package I sent you by yesterday's coach, everything requisite for painting: I have added to it the outline of a head, and on another sheet the rough sketch of the same head. Before you begin, you must know how to prepare the ivory, which is never sold in a state sufficiently polished or white. The process of whitening must be done by placing it on a moderately-heated oven, or in the sun, which will warp one side; turn it then on the other, and when it has the degree of whiteness you require, take it out, that it may not become too dry; for in that case it loses its transparency, and is apt to split when cut. This operation finished, you must proceed to one of more consequence and difficulty, and which requires practice: it is the polishing. Some painters use a large scratcher; others, an instrument with a blade three or four inches long, and of a triangular shape. To either of these I prefer the use of a razor: to benefit completely by it, you must be sure it have not the smallest notch in it, or that it be not too sharp. Open it so that the back part of the blade touches the handle; in that way you will use it easily to scrape your ivory from angle to angle. When you have thus polished the whole, begin again from the contrary angles, to be quite assured there remains no traces of the saw upon the side you wish to paint. I think I see you, good Ellen, in all the trouble of this process, of which I have no doubt you will acquit yourself with address and skill, although with a little impatience.

You say to yourself, might not this be purchased ready prepared, or done so to order? yes; often, but not always: besides, to be able to judge whether a thing be well done, you must know how to do it yourself. Continue therefore with courage your little undertakings, sweet Ellen, taking from out of that chest the band-box, which does not contain ribands, although resembling one for that use: open it; what you see there is a pounce-stone, pulverized and passed through a silk sieve. Place your ivory in the middle of the bottom of the box, holding it firm with one hand, while with the other you take that small bit of paper in the corner of the same box: use it to rub the pounce on the side of the ivory you have polished; being always careful to do it with a circular movement.

If your ivory be now of a dead white, and have lost the shine given to it by the razor, take it out of the box, holding it so that your fingers do not touch the surface, so troublesome to prepare, and brush off lightly with a painting brush any grits that may have adhered to it; for this purpose, take one of the largest hair pencils I have sent you: it may be serviceable to remove in the same way any specks or dust while you are painting. For inasmuch as these preliminary operations are disagreeable and even fatiguing, so much more comparatively will what remains to be done require neatness, attention, and care. To prove this to you, I will not scruple to repeat, so important it is, never to suffer your fingers to touch the ivory; hold it always at the extremities, for the colour will not settle in a place touched even by your fair and delicate hands. If, however, such an accident were to happen, as there is no evil without its remedy, be not quite driven to despair, but have recourse to the pumice-powder, and with a paper stump, rather pointed, gently rub the place where the sad misfortune has occurred. But, to avoid as much as possible a recurrence of such accidents, you must, when at work, take a sheet of paper to rest your hand upon, and when you shall use body-colour, have a piece of wood or pasteboard made (for the same purpose) in such a way that it touch not the miniature; for in consequence of the gum which is in the colours, the heat of the hand might cause the paper to stick to the painting. Your ivory at last prepared, and all accidents cautioned against, begin your work by placing this same ivory on your desk, in the middle, with a sheet of paper under it, and the sketch I sent you above.

By enumerating the names and properties of the different colours chiefly employed in miniature painting, I could still keep you in suspense, and further exercise your patience; but you shall lose nothing by a postponement, as I do not intend to spare you when more at leisure. In the mean time use the palette ready prepared with colours I send you, and study the plate annexed to this letter, in order to become acquainted with the names of the colours I have marked thereon. From amongst your sable hair pencils, choose one with a firm and sharp point, yet pliable, so as to enable you to produce with it clear decided lines; use it to make the outline of the head, and be careful not to load your pencil with more water than necessary to dilute a very small quantity of colour; take some carmine lake for that purpose; and if you wish to efface an incorrect stroke, do it with the point of a hair pencil, dipped in water only.

I postpone, until to-morrow, the directions you will require for the first shades; endeavour, at all events, to let your outline be as correct as possible.

From: L. Mansion, *Letters Upon the Art of Miniature Painting* (London: R. Ackerman, 1822), 22–28.

16

"Photography and Painting"

Some months ago we mentioned the union of photography and painting, the production of a finished miniature retaining the accuracy and tint of the Talbotype, the tone and shadows being greatly improved. M. Mansion, the artist associated with M. Claudet, has recently made farther progress in the application of the solar picture to aid the more ancient art. The metallic hue of the Daguerreotype, and the not much more agreeable brown colour of the Talbotype, have been and are the principal objections to these wonderful works of nature. The miniature-painting above referred to, on the photography itself, was intended to remove this objection, and with great success; but the colour is still brown. By the new method the truthfulness of the Talbotype is maintained, and the colour of life given to the portrait. The outlines are most accurately traced on a material invented by M. Mansion, and upon it he then paints a likeness. The specimens shewn to us – copies of landscapes, and of men and horses – were most minute resemblances. With a similar view, M. Claudet has been experimenting on Fizeau's process of etching Daguerreotypes, and we were greatly pleased with his advancement. Some of the impressions were exceedingly distinct, and the lights and shades as marked as in the ordinary engraving. In the fainter prints, however, – and the fainter the better for this purpose, – the likeness was sufficiently clear for M. Mansion to paint it to the life. So now any one may have a painted facsimile of a Talbotype, or a coloured impression of a Daguerreotype.

"Photography and Painting," *The Literary Gazette: A Weekly Journal of Literature, Science and the Fine Arts*, London, Issue 1512 (January 10, 1846), 38.

17

"Photography"

Henry Morley and William Wills

The den of the photographer, in which he goes through those mysterious operations which are not submitted to the observation of the sitter, is a small room lighted by a window, and communicating into a dark closet, veiled with heavy curtains. Our sense of the supernatural, always associated with dark closets, was excited strongly in this chamber, by the sound of a loud rumbling in the bowels of the house, and the visible departure of a portion of the wall to lower regions. We thought instinctively of bandits who wind victims up and down in moveable rooms or turn them up in treacherous screw bedsteads. But, of course, there was no danger to be apprehended. What we saw was, of course, only a contrivance to save labour in conveying pictures up and down for colouring or framing. Our consciences having been satisfied on this point, the expert magician took a plate of the prescribed size, made ready to his hand. Such plates consist of a thin layer of silver fixed upon copper, and are provided to the artist highly polished; but a final and superlative polish is given to each plate, with a "buff" or pad like a double handled razor strop, tinged with a fine mineral powder. Simple as it appears, the final polishing of the plate is an operation that can only succeed well under a practised pair of hands, that regulate their pressure by a refined sense of touch. The plate thus polished was brushed over finally and very lightly, as with the touch of a cat's paw, with a warm pad of black velvet freshly taken from an oven.

To witness the next process we went into the dark closet itself, the very head quarters of spectredom. There, having carefully excluded daylight, the operator lifted up the lid of a small bin, rapidly fixed the plate, silver side downwards, in a place made underneath for its reception, shut down the lid, and began to measure seconds by counting, talking between whiles, thus:- "One – that box – two – contains – three – chloride of iodine – four – strewn – five – six – at the bottom. Now!" (Presto, out came the plate in a twinkling, and was held against a sheet of white paper, upon which it reflected a ghastly straw colour by the light of a small jet of gas.) "Ah, tint not deep enough!" The plate was popped into its vapour bath again with magic quickness. "Seven – the action of the iodine" (continued the operator, counting seconds, and teaching us our lesson in the same breath) "rising in vapour upon the surface – eleven – of the plate – twelve – causes it to take in succession – thirteen – fourteen –fifteen – all the colours of the spectrum – sixteen – seventeen; and deposits upon it a film." As he went on solemnly counting, we asked how long he exposed the plate to the visitation of that potent vapour. "A very short time," he replied; "but it varies – thirty – thirty-one – according to the light in the next room – thirty-five – thirty-six – thirty-seven. Adjusting the plate to the weather, thirty-eight – is the result of an acquired instinct – thirty-nine – forty. Now it is ready." The plate was out, and its change to a deeper straw colour was shown. The lid of an adjoining bin was lifted, and the iodized plate was hung in the same way over another vapour; that of the chloride of bromine, that the wraiths of the two vapours might mingle, mingle, mingle as black spirits with white, blue spirits with gray. In this position it remained but a very short time, while we stood watching by in the dark cupboard. The plate having had its temper worked upon by these mysterious agencies was rendered so extremely sensitive, that it was requisite to confine it at once, in a dark hole or solitary cell, made ready for it in a wooden frame; a wooden slide was let down over it, and it was ready to be carried to the camera.

[. . .]

The frame was then inserted in its place, the slide removed, and the prepared silver reposing in the darkness was laid open to receive the meditated shock upon its sensibility. The sitters were requested then to close their eyes for a minute, that the eyelids might be rested, then to look fixedly in the direction indicated by a little picture pinned against a screen. Then "Now, quite still; try to look pleasant – a little pleasanter!" The cap was off, and the two figures, fixed as statues, shone upon the magic mirror in the camera, rigidly pleasant. In half a minute, – counted accurately by the operator – suddenly, the stopper was again clapped over the glass in front; the slide was let down over the tablet, upon which light, having done its work, must shine no more until the plate was light-proof. Mars and Venus in conjunction having entered the third house, we retired into the necromancer's den to observe what would follow.

[. . .]

Truly, a fine picture it is. The lady's dress suggests upon the plate as much delicate workmanship as would have given labour for a month to the most skilful of painters. The lilies that we did not like upon the cape, how exquisite they look here in the picture! But as this group was destined to be coloured, we were courteously invited to the colouring room, a tiny closet in which two damsels were busily at work, one upon a lady's dress, the other upon the forehead of a gentleman, putting in the yellow rather lavishly, but with a good effect. "The faces," she informed us, "must be coloured strongly, or they will be put out by the bright blue sky." We pointed to a small box labelled "Sky," remarking that the fair painters were magicians, to carry the sky in a wafer-box. To which one of them promptly answered "Yes; and Ogres, too, for that pill-box contains gentlemen's and ladies' 'Flesh.'"

These terrific creatures – who had quite the ways of damsels able to eat rice pudding in an honest manner – then made us acquainted with a few dry facts. The colours used by them were all dry minerals, and were laid on with the fine point of a dry brush; pointed between the lips, and left to become dry before using. A little rubbing caused these tints to adhere to the minute pores upon the plate. Each colour was of course rubbed on with its own brush, and so expertly, that a large plate very elaborately painted, with a great deal of unquestionable taste, had been, as we were told, the work only of an hour. On a subsequent occasion, we saw in the same room our picture of the Doctor under the painter's hands, and undergoing flattery. We admired the subdued tone which the artist had, as we thought, taken the wise liberty of giving to the glare of the red coat. "Yes," she replied, "but I must make it redder presently; when we don't paint coats bright enough, people complain. They tell us that we make them look as if they wore old clothes."

[. . .]

The rays that have passed through to form the picture, have been called the photogenic rays: they refract not quite in the same way as the luminous or colorific rays, and therefore the focus of the photogenic picture and that of the picture thrown on the ground glass will not exactly coincide. For this, allowance has to be made in practice, and accurate instruments for ascertaining the true photogenic focus have been invented, one by M. Claudet, and another by Mr. G. Knight. They are called Focimeters. There are hidden mysteries, however, connected with this portion of the subject. Means have been already here and there discovered, by which the colours of the spectrum may be printed at once on photographic tablets, and the sun – most brilliant of artists – may paint his pictures at the same time that he is engraving them [...] A new material is said to have been introduced in aid of this effect. While all mechanical details have been perfected, we may therefore expect this new step to be made publicly, by which Apollo will be raised above Apelles in the world of art.

From: Henry Morley (1822–1894) and William Wills (1810–1880), "Photography," *Household Words*, March 19, 1853; 7, Iss. 156, 54–61, 56–60.

18

A Manual of Artistic Colouring, as applied to Photographs

Alfred H. Wall

Chapter VII
Colouring with Dry or Powder Colours.

Daguerreotypes and glass positives are generally coloured by a very easy process with dry brushes and powder-colours, by the aid of which some of our more skilful operators produce effects closely allied to those of coloured crayons.

The method of manipulation is so very simple that, save in the selection of tints and colours, there is not much to teach, and consequently not much to be mastered by the pupil in the shape of mechanical difficulties. Until very recently, powder-colours were prepared with so little reference to the surface to which they were intended to adhere, that this branch of photographic colouring occupied a very insignificant position; and the only directions of a *practical nature* that could be given for their use, were simply to *dust* on a little pink or flesh colour here, and *dust* it carefully off there, blow it gently to remove the *very* loose particles, and – that was all: the powder once on in the form of *dust* of a certain colour could not be retouched, because every attempt to add more colour merely removed that already applied. Under these circumstances, it was only colourists who prepared their own pigments with a knowledge of the peculiar requirements of this process, and the means of meeting them, who were really successful.

Now, however, if the amateur meet with such difficulties, it is his own fault; for although bad powder-colours are very extensively sold, some of our best colour manufacturers have undertaken their preparation, and thus bestow a really artistic power in their application to the collodion or silver surface. I find in practice that the colours are best applied before and after varnishing.

The Materials

The colours are sold in small bottles, and their tints and shades are indicated by names (suggestive of their use) and numbers. If a box of these be purchased it will be provided with a set of earthenware saucers to contain the colours, or a palette of velvet for the same purpose, brushes, gold and silver shells, &c.

The brushes or pencils should be carefully selected. In oil or water a somewhat inferior brush, being aided by moisture, may do; but the dry brush will not retain its point unless it be of good material and carefully made. As softness is one of their most desirable qualities, the *dark* and not the red French sables will be found best. They must be carefully preserved from dust, well rinsed after use, and pointed with the lips before being put aside to dry. It is desirable to keep a good supply of brushes, as they soon lose their fine point when in use, and this can only be recovered by moisture, after which they are not again fit for service until *perfectly* dry. A camel-hair brush, called a "duster," will also be required.

The Blower. – An india-rubber bottle with an ivory mouth-piece, used to remove loose superfluous colour.

Varnishes, &c. – A varnish prepared expressly for the reception of dry colours should be selected, as very few indeed of ordinary varnishes (if any) take the powders well, being too hard and smooth. A varnish for coloured glass positives is needed to be something more than a brilliant transparent protection to the film. Many of the ordinary positive varnishes serve the protective purpose perfectly enough, but they are worse than useless for the purpose of the colourist, who requires a surface to which his powder colours will adhere when properly applied. The majority of the varnishes are, as I have said, too hard and glassy; whilst some few, into which Canada balsam and turpentine enter, do not set properly, but are tacky, and cause the colour to adhere in patches. They, moreover, rapidly discolour. Select, then, a varnish which does not lower the whites of the picture much, and which, instead of presenting a smooth glassy surface, affords sufficient texture to which the colours may adhere. A black varnish is sometimes used for "baking up" the glass positives, the principal effect of which is the utter destruction of depth and transparency in the shadows, the changing of the purest whites into leaden gray, and the imparting of a dull, heavy, and metallic appearance to the whole picture: such a photograph will *never colour well.* The best material for "backing up" is a dark maroon velvet, which having depth in itself *and colour,* is no small assistance both to the photograph and the colouring.

The First Colouring

Your picture duly selected, with a clean, well pointed, and *quite dry* pencil, take up very little colour, and apply it with a *gentle* rubbing motion in a circular direction. As is usual, commence with –

The Face

Take up the pale orange, or the "horizon tint," and mix with a little white: with this colour (a pale, warm yellow) strengthen the high lights (see Maxim 40) which will be found upon such portions as are most prominently exposed to the more direct rays of the light, such being of course the top of the brow, the cheek bones, and the nose, and chin, upon the lighted side of the face: soften this into the "local" tint of the flesh, which may be represented by either of the prepared "flesh tints," with or without the addition of a little warm brown, orange, or carmine, as the complexion to be imitated may determine. Darken the local tint as you approach the half-tones, carefully avoiding the *darkest* shadows, which *the powder colours always destroy*. Where the skin is thin the blue veins will tinge the flesh with their own colour, therefore touch a little pale blue upon the corner, between the eye and the nose, the temple, &c.: a stronger blue, green, or purplish gray, if your subject be a man, may be required about the upper and lower jar. With careful touches, colour the lightest part of the upper lip with a little crimson, and that of the lower lip with pink, finishing it with carmine. If the eye be blue or brown, put a touch of either colour, *with extreme care*, into the iris diagonally opposite the "spark" or gleam of strong light in the eye (see Maxim 45). Should the hair be light, a little of the requisite colour may be worked over the lighter portions.

[. . .]

Scarlet Coats and Jewellery

In colouring a scarlet coat with powder colours, your great difficulty will be found in preserving its folds and roundness; the opaque nature of your pigments[1] destroying the half-tints and shadows in the same degree as they produce the force and brilliancy demanded of a truthful effect. In this case, therefore, more than common care is requisite. Select a colour for your high lights first. This should be a scarlet of a somewhat orange tone; and be careful that in obtaining it you use *no white*, which would effectively destroy the purity and beauty of your colour. The next colour is the local one, viz., scarlet; the next, carmine: and the shadows are coloured with crimson, which, upon *the darkest shades*, should be applied *before varnishing only*. You will find that the local scarlet is a colour somewhat difficult to meet with.

Jewellery is too generally touched with the gold and silver sold in shells, which, unless used with no little skill, produce a very coarse and untruthful appearance. The simple fact of the jewellery thus touched having lights and shadows of its own continually varying with the light in which the picture may be placed, and perfectly independent of the light and shade upon the image itself, should denounce the vulgar taste displayed in its use, and confine it to the studios of a class of "photographic artists" who laud the fact of its being "real gold" to their sitters, as an inducement for the outlay of "tuppence" more for a ring, or "sixpence" for "a gold chain." I have seen a minute touch of the silver applied with singularly good effect to the spark of light in the eye, but it perishes as the silver blackens. *Gold* is best executed with water or oil colours. In this case take Naples yellow for the high lights, yellow ochre for the local colour, bistre and burnt sienna for the shadows, and orange chrome or deep cadmium for the reflected lights. *Diamond*s are best represented by a vividly bright touch of pure white (water colour), and coloured stones by the same upon the local colour, opposite a touch of this local colour mixed with white, to represent the transparency. For *silver,* use white for the lights upon a ground of warm pale grey, with somewhat warmer shadows. For *pearls*, use a brilliant touch of white, very minute, diagonally opposite another similar touch of white and Naples yellow. *Coral* may be painted in with lake and vermilion for the local colour; pure lake for the shadows, and pure vermilion for the lights; the highest lights with the same and a little white.

The Use of Water Colours

Upon glass positives water colours should be seldom used, as their effect upon such surfaces will always be strikingly inharmonious and offensive to good taste (although a touch or two may sometimes be carefully applied to produce the sparkling high lights of jewellery, lace &c., as I have already stated), and are also, as I shall explain, necessary in the treatment of certain defects.

To colour and improve an Inferior Positive

To do this may very frequently (as in the case of a bad picture being the sole relic of a deceased relative or friend) be most desirable. Suppose, then, we have before us one of those leaden-hued ghostly positives, which somebody has bought very dearly at an exceedingly low price. Here it is in all its ugliness, either pallid and indefinite in a thick white fog, or sooty and begrimmed in a black one. Suppose it to be the former. In the first place, if necessary, we "put in the eyes," with a fine sable pencil and a little Indian ink, carefully strengthening the line around the iris, and touching in the pupil with a neat clean touch; the eyelids and lashes may be marked with the same, and, if required, the nostrils and line dividing the lips also. This done, take the powder colours, and with a little of the dark gray, strengthen the barely visible half-tints, doing the same for the lights with the white, being careful *not to touch the wet with the dry colours*, as the latter would adhere to the former far more strongly than to the collodion surface, and would not admit of softening. The hair may be strengthened with the Indian ink, and then the varnish can be applied; after which, proceed to colour as usual.

And now suppose we have the "under-developed" and "under-exposed" positive (the black one) to operate upon.

The sockets of the eyes are a dense black mass, in which the optics are nearly entirely lost. To bring them out, use Indian ink and Chinese white (water colours) – the former for the markings or drawing of the eye; the latter, with *very* light careful touches, for the lights and white portion of the eye. Next, take your dry white and work it into the high lights, and, mixed with a little gray, into the half-tints, until the image begins to show some little signs of roundness, although it will now appear a very coarse chalky smudge. After this, varnish and colour as usual.

But although thus much may be done to remedy these defects, *such* productions cannot be *much* improved upon.

Author's Note

1 To claim transparency for powder colours, in themselves, is a common mistake. When ground to an impalpable powder and slightly applied, they, by the fineness of their particles, *seem* almost transparent, but of course cannot be really so.

From: Alfred H. Wall, *A Manual of Artistic Colouring, as applied to Photographs. A Practical Guide to Artists and Photographers* (London: Thomas Piper, 1861), 75–86.

19

"Colouring Photographs. –No. I."

A very profitable and pleasing occupation has followed upon the development of the art of photography, by the necessity which exists to colour those portraits taken by the *camera*, where a closer resemblance to miniature painting is desirable. The delicate handling and more refined manipulation of the female hand has been found to be pre-eminently suited to this interesting pursuit, and consequently ladies far outnumber male artists in this speciality. The remuneration, of course, varies according to the talent of the pencil to which the portraits are confided, and sums of a very liberal character are given to the more highly gifted. The extent of these gifts is soon detected by the photographer, who thus makes a judicious selection of his human aids, and distributes his works according to the prices he expects to receive from his sitters. In this way many hundreds of ladies are engaged, and a more appropriate and suitable avocation, or one which may more gradually tend to excellence in its department, can scarcely be conceived. It is incumbent, however, that the followers of this art should understand something of drawing, and according to their advancement in this particular, and their judicious recognition of the harmony of colour, is the measure of their comparative fitness for this new means of employment. At first blush it might be supposed that a knowledge of colouring alone is all that is requisite, but this would be an error of a very grave nature. Painting, it should be borne in mind, is only drawing with a soft point, and, therefore, the mere laying in of tints, or flat grounds, as observable in the colouring of prints or maps, is not drawing, or any art at all, but only a mechanical dexterity, requiring but a little practice to obtain perfection, beyond which, in contradistinction to art, the hand cannot go. Those, therefore, who would expect to treat a photograph as they would a print, would find themselves most deplorably at fault, although it is true that there are some *cartes de visites,* and a few of the larger photographs themselves, which merely receive a wash, or application of wet or dry colour, requiring little or no talent beyond the most rudimentary knowledge of applying the tint. On the other hand, those photographs which require to be converted into the similitude of highly-finished miniatures, necessitate the exercise of most of the claims of art, for although the outline and detail are there as guides, this outline and detail in the lights is soon lost under the opaque colours, which are necessarily used. The departure of a hair's breadth is enough to destroy the expression, and mayhap put the mouth or eyes out of drawing, and then the hand that is not sufficiently instructed, in its attempts to recover the missing exactitude, will most assuredly get inextricably confounded, and the utter spoliation of the whole affair must result.

From our few last sentences it would, perhaps, be conceived that, in the colouring of photographs, only those ladies who are educated as artists, or who possess an art-feeling, will find employment. We do not, however, mean to convey any such restricted notion. We mean to say, on the contrary, that, from the simple process, accessible to most, of tinting photographic likenesses with a wash of transparent colour, to the highest aspirations, where a finish of microscopic effect, added to breadth of light and shade, is desiderated – a very wide space for different orders of talent – ladies may find an occupation for their time, in which, as in all other branches of remunerative industry, the best work demands and receives the best pay. But while we take this comprehensive view of the matter, it must be necessarily understood that our future remarks apply alone to those ladies who are already acquainted with drawing, and, this accepted, we will endeavour to convey to them the easiest and shortest method of painting photographs to resemble miniatures; nor is it our intention to repeat those general rules and precepts known to all and followed by so few. This display of erudition might dazzle some, weary others, but would be useful to none. Our ambition is to render service to young lady artists, and to answer, to the extent of our ability, the many applications which have been, and may be, made to us by those amateurs who are desirous of following this elegant path in which art and science, figuratively, if not literally, go hand in hand and *vis a vis*.

Passing over the process of tinting with dry colouring, which is done with a brush and powdered chalks, the clouds and background being effected more boldly and freely with a "stump," we arrive at once at the operation of painting photographs in water colours. These are composed principally of transparent colours; but semi-transparent and opaque colours – the latter better known as body colours, and generally restricted to white – are likewise employed. The flesh palette is composed of white, lamp-black, bistre, yellow ochre, ultramarine, carmine lake, burnt sienna, Indian yellow, Indian red, Chinese vermillion, lake, carmine lake mixed with lamp-black and a larger quantity of gum arabic, a mixture of vandyke brown with burnt sienna. In miniature painting, a sharp, firm, yet pliable sable-hair pencil is chosen, so that clear, decisive lines are produced. This is used to follow the outline of the head, and great care should be used not to load the pencil with more water than is necessary to dilute a very small quantity of colour. Amongst the pencils there should be three different kinds. Those which have their points square are intended for body colour; the second should be made of squirrel's or camel's hair, for sketching the flesh, the groundwork, and the draperies, executed in transparent colours; the third should be of sable-hair, and are used to polish or blend the painting, and give the finishing touches.

Begin with the strongest shades of the head, and while following out the forms be careful not to get the lines too hard. If, for instance, while painting the eyes, you mark the lid by too strong an outline, you will find it very difficult to soften it afterwards. The same may be observed relative to the eyelashes and the shades of the nose and chin. Begin, therefore, by sketching them lightly, with a due regard to the instructions of complexion as given to you, or the actual model who may be present. These parts must then be gone over several times till they have acquired the necessary strength. Care should be taken to use only warm colours at first, and the grey tints, which are always observable at the edge of the middle tints towards the side approaching the light, should be left until afterwards, otherwise that transparency which gives such force and roundness to the shadows, and lifts as it were the lighter parts reposing upon them, would be lost. The highest lights should be carefully preserved and kept broad, particularly those which are placed upon the upper part of the cheeks, the extremity of the nose, and the forehead. There are some who make use of a pen-knife with great success to scratch out the colour, but it requires skill, and you must employ only the edge of the blade, avoiding the point. It is, however, better to proceed carefully, to be obliged to add colour, rather than to take it off. The work should be done by hatching or etching, that is, by a series of short lines crossing each other like lattice, somewhat coarse at first, the repetitions over and over again serving to give that beautiful grain and finish as observable in the most approved miniatures. These lines should moreover follow the forms and dimples of the muscles of the face, and a close observation of a line engraving by William Finden or Strange, or indeed any good master of the burin, will explain at once what we mean. The brush thus, as it were, models the parts. If, notwithstanding all precautions, the colour is found too thick in some parts, or in consequence of taking too much water in the brush some blotted strokes are perceivable, the point of the brush dipped in water, with the slightest quantity of colour, will, if applied, dissolve it without entirely taking it away. It is essential to avoid working too long upon the same spot, for fear of disturbing the colours already put on.

The above may be sufficient for a first lesson, but we shall be glad to receive any inquiries upon the subject, trusting to do our best in removing any difficulty which may occur, by the clearness and perspicuity of our explanations.

"Colouring Photographs. –No. I." *The Lady's Newspaper & Pictorial Times* (London), Saturday January 31, 1863, vol. xxxiii, Issue 840, 244–245.

SECTION 5

"DIRECT" AND "INDIRECT" COLOR

20

"On the Application of Science to the Fine and Useful Arts. Heliochrome"

Robert Hunt

The name of *Heliochromy*, or sun-colouring, is very appropriately given to a process by which photographic pictures in their natural colours are obtained. The name originally proposed for sun-drawing by M. Niépce, was *Heliography*, which is, in every respect, far preferable to photography, which signifies light-drawing; whereas, we have every reason for believing that these pictures are produced by a principle associated with light, but which gives none, that is, it possesses no illuminating power.

The problem of the production of colour upon sensitive tablets, by the action of the radiations from the coloured surfaces of natural objects, the coloured copy corresponding with the hues of Nature, is now solved. We have previously stated (*Art-Journal*, p. 188) that M. E. Becquerel in Paris and Mr. Hill in the United States have succeeded in producing coloured pictures by the action of the solar rays upon metallic plates. The former published his process, the latter has not yet done so. Since that time, the nephew of M. Niépce, one of the earliest investigators of this important subject, has circulated specimens of the coloured pictures called by him *Heliochromy*, and we have had an opportunity of inspecting several of them – the personal gift of M. Niépce de Saint-Victor to Mr. Malone. There is something so exquisitely charming in these pictures – though the process is still imperfect, and the production of them involves such very important scientific considerations, that we are anxious to embrace the earliest opportunity of putting the readers of the *Art-Journal* in possession of all the facts of the progress of discovery, and such explanations of the process, and of the physical phenomena, as we are in possession of.

Without entering into the discussion which has been carried on for a long period, as to the phenomena of colour, it is necessary for the perfect understanding of the results obtained, that the chromatic conditions of a decomposed sunbeam should be clearly appreciated, and the relation of this coloured image to the chemical effects obtained, distinctly understood. A pencil of light is passed through a prism, and we obtain an elongated image consisting of a beautifully coloured set of bands. There are three primaries, red, yellow, and blue, which by inter-combination give rise to other tints, so that altogether we are acquainted with nine coloured rays, – crimson, red, orange, yellow, green, blue, indigo, violet and lavender. The colours of natural objects are produced by the decomposition of the rays of light, this being effected by some peculiar *surface* action. Now, if we expose a piece of photographic paper or a daguerreotype plate, to the action of this spectrum, or to the radiations from coloured surfaces, we shall find that the chemical effect has no relation to the intensity of light belonging to the coloured ray. For example, supposing the coloured image of the nine rays to fall upon a sensitive tablet, the result is of the following curious character:- One of the red rays protects the paper from all change, the other usually makes a *red* impression; the orange and yellow rays have no chemical action, though these have the most illuminating power. The chemical action commences in the green ray, rapidly increases in energy in the blue, and exerts its maximum power over the space covered by the indigo, violet, and lavender, still continuing with much energy over a space beyond the lavender, in which no light can be detected.

[...]

By far the most important investigation has been carried out by M. Niépce de Saint-Victor, an abstract of whose *Mémoire* we hasten to communicate to readers of the *Art-Journal.*

The memoir is entitled, "Upon the relation existing between the colours of certain coloured flames, with the Heliographic images coloured by light."

When a plate of silver is plunged into a solution of sulphate of copper and chloride of sodium, at the same time that it is rendered *Electro-positive* by means of the voltaic battery, the chloride formed becomes susceptible of coloration, when having been withdrawn from the bath, it receives the influence of light. This was the discovery of M. Edmond Becquerel: M. Saint-Victor, had been led to think that a relation existed between the colour communicated by a body to a flame, and the colour developed upon a plate of silver, which should have been chloridated with the body which colours this flame.

The bath in which the plate of silver was plunged, was formed of water saturated with chlorine, to which was added a chloride possessing the property of colouring flame.

It is well known that strontian gives a *purple* colour to flames in general, and to that of alcohol in particular. If we prepare a plate of silver and pass it into water saturated with chlorine, to which is added some chloride of strontian, and when thus prepared we place *upon it* a coloured design, of red and other colours, and then expose it to the sunshine, after six or seven minutes we shall perceive that the colours of the image are reproduced upon the plate, but the reds much more decidedly than the others. When we would produce successfully the other rays of the solar spectrum, we operate in the same manner as we have indicated for the red ray, employing for the *orange* the chloride of calcium, or that of uranium for the *yellow*, or hypochlorite of soda, or the chlorides of sodium and potassium. If we plunge a plate of silver into the chlorine liquid, or if we expose the plate to the vapour we obtain all the colours by the light, but the yellow only with any degree of vivacity. Very fine yellows have been obtained with a bath composed of water slightly acidulated with muriatic acid with a salt of copper.

The green rays are obtained with boracic acid or the chloride of nickel; also with all the salts of copper.

The blue rays are obtained with the double chloride of copper and ammonia. Indigo rays are obtained with the same substance.

The violet rays are obtained with the chloride of strontian and the sulphate of copper.

All the substances which give coloured flames give also coloured images by light. If we take any of the substances which do not give colour to flame we do not obtain coloured images by the light; we produce upon the plate a negative image composed merely of black and white as in the ordinary photographs. Those substances which give white flames, as the chloride of antimony, the chlorate of lead, and the chloride of zinc, yield no colour by luminous action. All the colours of a picture have been produced by preparing a bath composed of the deuto-chloride of copper; and Niépce states that this salt, thrown into burning alcohol, produces a variegated flame according to the intensity of the fire; and it is nearly the same with all the salts of copper mixed with chlorine.

[. . .]

If we form a bath composed of all the substances which separately give a dominant colour, we obtain very lively colours; but the great difficulty is the mixing in proper proportions, for it happens nearly always that some colours are found excluded by others. By care, however, we ought to arrive at the reproduction of all the colours. There exist many difficulties, more indeed than in any of the ordinary processes of photography. We cannot always depend upon obtaining the same results with the same materials, owing principally to the difficulty of preserving the solution at a uniform strength. Liquid chlorine is necessary, the application of dry chlorine will not produce the same result. The action of heat upon these prepared plates is, in some respects, analogous to the effects of light. By warming a plate over a spirit-lamp we produce successfully the following tints – brown red; a cerise red; scarlet; and red having a whitish tint.

Numerous experiments have been made by Saint-Victor to produce the colours upon the salts of silver and copper spread on paper, but hitherto without success; a metallic plate of silver – the plated copper answers – must be employed.

Iodine and bromine, and their salts, have been tried, but they will not produce a surface capable of developing colours. Chlorine, in the state of chlorates or chlorides, is the only substance which possesses the property of being coloured by light, when chemically combined with metallic silver.

The mode of operating recommended is, to form a bath with one-fourth by weight of the chloride, and three-fourths of water. When the muriatic acid is used with a salt of copper, we must add one one-tenth of water. When the bath is composed of several substances, it is essential to filter the solution carefully, so as to obtain very transparent solutions, and it must be preserved in a well stoppered bottle.

The quantity necessary to prepare two or more plates should always be taken, because the bath is weakened considerably at each operation; it can, however, be rendered active by the addition of a few drops of muriatic acid.

The purer the silver employed, the more perfect is the impression, and the more intense the colours.

The plate being very highly polished, which is best effected by tripoli powder and ammonia, is connected with the battery and then plunged into the bath, and kept there for some minutes; it is then taken from the bath, washed in a large quantity of water, and dried over a spirit-lamp. The surface thus produced is a dull neutral tint, often almost black, and upon exposing it to the light, the colours are produced by removing the blackness; the surface is, in fact, *eaten out in colours.* The sensibility of the plate appears to be increased by the action of heat, and when brought by the spirit-lamp to the cerise red colour it is in its most sensitive state. At present, however, the plates cannot be rendered very sensitive, two or three hours being required to produce a decided effect in the camera obscura. It is, however, already found that the fluoride of sodium will very much accelerate the operation.

The fixation of the coloured image is, however, still a point of considerable difficulty, and although a certain degree of permanence has been recovered, the colours fade out by exposure, and eventually pass away. A kind of lacquer appears to have been applied to the plates we have seen, and ordinary diffused light does not seem to produce much change upon them.

Such is an outline of the researches of M. Niépce de Saint-Victor, as communicated by him to the Academy of Sciences – he is still zealously occupied in the enquiry, and we hope very shortly to be enabled to communicate some yet more important results. The problem is, however, solved; we can produce pictures by the agency of the solar beam in natural colours; that principle which gives to the exterior creation the charm of colour, will so regulate the chemical agency of the actinic power with which it is associated, that, on properly prepared surfaces, the images are painted in their native hues. The heliochromes will, we have no doubt, in a short time enable the artist to catch the ever-varying tints of nature, and preserve them as studies. This is certainly one of the greatest steps made in photography.

From: Robert Hunt, "On the Application of Science to the Fine and Useful Arts." "Heliochrome," *The Art Journal*, October 1851, 257–258.

21

"Those who Live in Glass Houses"

"THOSE WHO LIVE IN GLASS HOUSES—SHOULD not throw stones," says the adage. But who ever *did* live in glass-houses before the days of Sir Joseph Paxton or the invention of photography? And why were they expected to be constantly pelting their neighbours? Has the sun necessarily a combative effect upon dwellers in those traps to catch sunbeams?

I, who live in a glass-house all day, am inclined to answer the last question in the affirmative, when aggravated by ugly or capricious sitters. May I therefore, a humble photographer, venture one or two hints to the owners of countenances who desire them to be gracefully and accurately copied, and to those who try to copy them?

In turning over the leaves of an album, we frequently pass our acquaintances without even a nod. How is this? The photograph may be irreproachable as a work of art, and it is impossible to be other than a transcript of what was presented to the camera. How comes it, then, that it is not a likeness? Simply because the original was, at the critical moment, unlike himself. When about to be photographed, one is apt to feel that, like Marshal Ney,[1] the eyes of Europe are upon him – that, according to the position which he assumes, judgement will be passed on his good or bad figure, awkwardness or grace. He wishes to present himself on paper to an admiring, not to a critical, public. A nervous consciousness, moreover, that perhaps a guinea or two is involved in the operation, tends materially to add to his discomfiture. Trivial as this consideration may appear, it exerts a far greater influence on the expression than most persons are willing to acknowledge, even to themselves. Placed in a position always chosen by the operator (being, to save himself the trouble of rearranging accessories, precisely the same as that which the last sitter occupied), his head screwed into a vice behind, he is told to look at an indicated spot on the wall, and keep still. Thus posed, he regards further operations with much the same feelings of distrust as he would those of a dentist. In imagination, he hears the sharp rattle of the forceps, or the punch. His breathing becomes thicker and quicker as the critical moment arrives, his heart beats audibly against his waistcoat, and a hazy film falls over his eyes. In this delightful condition of mind and body, he is enjoined to "keep quite still, and put on a natural expression;" as if expressions were as easy to put on as gloves. The inevitable consequence is, that he "grins horribly with a ghastly smile," the like of which never passed over his features before. Yet both operator and sitter wonder why the portrait is so very unlike.

"I should like to have a landscape background for my portrait, if you please," is a frequent, but most inconsistent request. What can be more preposterous than to see a lady in full evening costume, quietly seated in a luxurious easy-chair, in the middle of a mountain pass, with a roaring cataract rushing madly down within a couple of inches of her immaculate book-muslin? The rugged pinnacle to which she is supposed to have flown (in her easy-chair) being carefully adapted to her satin shoes by a Brussels carpet, from which a tree is vigorously springing.

[. . .]

A lady or gentleman, having made up her or his mind to be photographed, naturally considers, in the first place, how to be dressed so as to show off to the best advantage. This is by no means such an unimportant matter as many might imagine. Let me offer a few words of advice touching dress. Orange colour, for certain optical reasons, is, photographically, black. Blue is white; other shades or tones of colour are proportionately darker or lighter, as they contain more or less of these colours. The progressive scale of photographic colour commences with the lightest. The order stands thus: white, light-blue, violet, pink, mauve, dark-blue, lemon, blue-green, leather-brown, drab, cerise, magenta, yellow-green, dark-brown, purple, red, amber, morone, orange, dead-black. Complexion has to be much considered in connexion with dress. Blondes can wear much lighter colours than brunettes; the latter always present better pictures in dark dresses, but neither look well in positive white. Violent contrasts of colour should be especially guarded against.

In photography, brunettes possess a great advantage over their fairer sisters. The lovely golden tresses lose all their transparent brilliancy, and are represented black; whilst the "bonnie blue e'e," theme of rapture to the poet, is misery to the photographer; for it is put entirely out. The simplest and most effective way of removing the yellow colour from the hair, is to powder it nearly white; it is thus brought to about the same photographic tint as in nature. The same rule, of course, applies to complexions. A freckle quite invisible at a short distance, is, on account of its yellow colour, rendered most painfully distinct when photographed. The puff-box must be called in to the assistance of art. Here let me intrude one word of general advice. Blue, as we have seen, is the most readily affected by light, and yellow the least; if, therefore, you would keep your complexion clear, and free from tan and freckles whilst taking your delightful rambles at the sea-side, discard by all means the blue veil, and substitute a dark green or yellow one in its stead. Blue tulle offers no more obstruction to the actinic rays of the sun than white. Half a yard of yellow net, though, perhaps, not very becoming, will be found more efficacious and considerably cheaper than a quart of Kalydor.[2] The cause of freckles is simple enough. It is nothing more than a darkening of the salts of iron contained in the blood, by the action of light. A freckled face is, therefore, an animated photograph.

Editor's Notes

1 Marshall Michel Ney (1769–1815) was one of Napoleon's main commanders, seeing service through the French Revolution and the Napoleonic Wars.

2 Rowland's 'Kalydor', on the market from the 1820s, was a lotion for the sun that "removes freckles, tan, sunburn, redness and roughness."

From: "Those who Live in Glass Houses," *All the Year Round*, November 26, 1864, Vol. XII, no. 292, 372–374.

22

"Colour Photography"

Gabriel Lippmann

The problem of colour photography is as old as photography itself. The desire of fixing the colours as well as the design of the beautiful image thrown on the screen of the camera, very naturally occurred to the earliest observers. Since the beginning of this century three distinct solutions to the problem have been realised.

The first solution, not quite a complete one, is founded on the peculiar properties of a silver compound, the violet subchloride of silver. E. Becquerel (1860) converted the surface of a daguerreotype plate into this silver compound, and by projecting on it the image of the solar spectrum, and other objects, obtained good coloured impressions. Poitevin substituted paper for the silver plate as a substratum. No other substance has been discovered that can play the part of the subchloride of silver. Moreover, the image is not fixed, in the photographic sense of the word; that is, the coloured impression is retained for any length of time in the dark, but it is blotted out by the action of daylight. The reason of it is this: the Becquerel images are formed by coloured silver-compounds, which remain sensible to light; so that they are destroyed by the continued action of light, in virtue of the same action which gave them birth. Despite the numerous experiments made by Becquerel, Poitevin, Zenther, and others, no substance has been found that is capable of destroying the sensibility of the subchloride for light without at the same time destroying its colour.

The second method for colour photography is an indirect one, and may be called the three-color method. It was invented in France by Ch. Cros, and at the same time by M. Ducos du Hauron (1869). German authorities claim the priority of the idea for Baron Bonstetten. Three separate negatives (colourless) are taken of an object, through three coloured screens. From these three positives (equally colourless) are made; and, lastly, the colour is supplied to these positives by means of aniline dyes or coloured inks. Thus three coloured monochromatic positives are obtained, which by superposition give a coloured image of the model. In the ingenious process lately invented by Prof. Joly, the three negatives, and apparently the corresponding three positives, are obtained interwoven on one and the same plate. The three-coloured method can give a very good approximation to the truth, and has probably a great future before it. We may call it, nevertheless, an indirect method, since the colours are not generated by the action of light, but are later supplied by the application of aniline dyes or other pigments. Moreover, the choice of these pigments, as well as of the coloured screens through which the negatives have been obtained, is in some degree an arbitrary choice.

The third and latest method by which colour photography has been realised is the interferential method, which I published in 1891, and the results of which I beg to lay before you this evening. It gives fixed images, the colours of which are due to the direct action of the luminous rays.

For obtaining coloured photographs by this method, only two conditions are to be fulfilled. We want (I) a transparent grainless photographic film of any kind, capable of giving a colourless fixed image by the usual means; and (2) we want a metallic mirror, placed in immediate contact with the film during the time of exposition.

A mirror is easily formed by means of mercury. The photographic plate being first enclosed in a camera-slide, a quantity of mercury is allowed to flow in behind the plate from this small reservoir, which is connected with the slide by a piece of india-rubber tubing.* The slide is then adapted to the camera, and the action of the light allowed to take place. After exposure the slide is separated from the camera, the mercury reservoir lowered so as to allow the mercury to flow back into it; the photographic plate is then taken out, developed and fixed. When dry, and examined by reflected light, it appears brilliantly coloured.

The sensitive film may be made either of chloride, iodide, or bromide of silver, contained in a substratum either of albumen, collodion, or gelatine. The corresponding developers, either acid or alkaline, have to be applied; the fixation may be cyanide or bromide of potassium. All these processes I have tried with success. For instance, the photograph of the electric spectrum now projected before your eyes, has been made on a layer of gelatino-bromide of silver, developed with amidol, and fixed with cyanide of potassium.

As you see, bright colour photographs may be obtained without changing the technique of ordinary photography; the same films, developers and fixators have to be employed; even the secondary operations of intensification and of isochromatisation are made use of with full success. The presence of the mirror behind the film during exposure makes the whole difference. From a chemical point of view nothing is changed, the result being a deposit of reduced silver left in the film, a brownish, colourless deposit. And yet the presence of a mirror during exposure causes the colourless deposit to show bright colours. Of course we want to know how this is done; we require to understand the theory of those colours.

We all know that colourless soap-water gives brilliant soap-bubbles; the iridescence of mother-of-pearl takes birth in colourless carbonate of lime; the gorgeous hues of tropical birds are simply reflected from the brownish substance which forms the feathers. Newton discovered the theory of these phenomena, and subjected them to measurement; he invented for the purpose the experiment called by the name of Newton's rings. Newton showed, as you know, that when two parallel reflecting surfaces are separated by a very short interval, and illumined by white light, they reflect only one of the coloured rays which are the constituents of white light. If, for instance, the interval between the reflecting surface is only two 10,000ths of a millimetre, violet rays are alone reflected, the rest being destroyed by interference; that is, the two surfaces send back two reflected rays whose vibrations interfere with one another, so as to destroy every vibration except that which constitutes violet light. If the interval between the reflecting surfaces be augmented to three 10,000ths of a millimetre, the destruction of vibration takes place for every vibration except that of red light, which alone remains visible in this case.

[. . . .]

How are we now to prove that the above theory is really applicable to the colour photograph you have seen? How can we demonstrate that those bright colours are due not to pigments, but to interference, as in the case of soap-bubbles? We have several ways of proving it.

First of all, we are not bound to the use of a peculiar chemical substance, such as Becquerel's subchloride of silver; we obtain colours with a variety of chemicals. We can, for instance, dispense entirely with the use of a silver salt; a film of gelatine or coagulated albumen impregnated with bichromate of potash, then washed with pure water after exposure, gives a very brilliant image of the spectrum.

Secondly, the colours on the plate are visible only in the direction of specular reflection. The position of the source by which we illumine the photograph being given, we have to put the eye in a corresponding position, so as to catch the regularly reflected rays. In every other position we see nothing but a colourless negative. Now, as you are aware, the colours of pigments are seen in any direction. By projecting again a photograph of the spectrum, and turning it to and fro, I can show you that the colours are visible only in one direction.

Thirdly, if we change the incidence of the illuminating rays, that is, if we look at the plate first in a normal direction, then more and more slantingly, we find that the colours change with the incidence exactly as they do in the case of soap-bubbles, or of Newton's rings; they change according to the same law, and for the same reasons. The red end of the spectrum turns successively to orange, yellow, green, blue, and violet. The whole system of colours, the image of the spectrum, is seen to move down into the part impressed by the infra-red. This is what we expect to happen with interference colours, and what again we cannot obtain with pigments.

Fourthly, if while looking at the film normally, we suffer it to absorb moisture – this can be done by breathing repeatedly on its surface – we see that the colours again change, but in an order opposite to that above described. Here the blue end of the spectrum is seen to turn gradually green, yellow, orange, red, and finally infra-red, that is, invisible. The spectrum this time seems to move up into the ultra-violet part of the improved film. By suffering the water to evaporate, the whole image moves back into its proper place; this experiment may be repeated any number of times.

[...]

It is necessary to use a transparent film, since an opaque one, such as is commonly in use, would hide the mirror from view; the sensitive substance must be grainless, or, at least, the grains must be much finer than the dimensions of the strata they are intended to form, and therefore wholly invisible. The preparation of transparent layers gave me at first much trouble; I despaired for years to find a proper method for making them. The method, however, is simply thus: if the sensitive substance (the silver bromide, for instance) be formed in presence of a sufficient quantity of organic matter, such as albumen, gelatine, or collodion, if it does not appear as a precipitate; it remains invisible; it *is* formed, but seems to remain dissolved in the organic substratum. If, for instance, we prepare a film of albumeno-iodide in the usual way, only taking care to lessen the proportions of iodide to half per cent of the albumen, we get a perfectly transparent plate, adapted to colour photography.

We want now to go a step further. It is very well for physicists to be contented with working on the spectrum, since that contains the elements of every compound colour; but we all desire to be able to photograph other objects than the spectrum – common objects with the most compound colours. We have again to take theory as a guide, and that tells us that the same process is able to give us either simple or compound colours. We have then to take a transparent and correctly isochromatised film, expose it with its mercury backing, then develop and fix it in the usual way; the plate, after drying, gives a correct coloured image of the objects placed before the camera. Only one exposure, only one operation is necessary for getting an image with every colour complete.

[...]

That the colours here observed are due to interference, and not to the presence of pigments, can be shown in the same way as with the spectrum. Here, again, we observe that the colours are visible only in the direction of specular reflection, that they change with the angle of incidence, that they change and disappear by wetting, and reappear by drying. Pigments remain equally visible and unaltered in colour under every incidence. If we attempted to touch up one of our photographs with oil or water-colours, the adulterated place would stand out on a colourless background by merely obscuring by diffused light. It is therefore impossible either to imitate or touch up a colour photograph made by the above described interferential method.

From: Gabriel Lippmann, "Colour Photography," *Nature*, April 30, 1896, vol. 53, no. 1383, 617–618.

23

"The Spectrum Plate. Theory: Practice: Result"

Sarah Angelina Acland

The point at which we all aim in ordinary photography is, I suppose, the representation in the greatest perfection possible of a coloured object in a monochrome print. How is this best obtained?

Mr. Cadett, in his pamphlet on "Orthochromatic Photography Simplified," says that all plates are sensitive to the visible rays of the spectrum, but the curve of sensitiveness is widely different from the curve showing the luminosities of the spectrum of white light. In a photograph of the spectrum on an ordinary plate, the action of light is greatest not where it is wanted – in the yellow – but in the blue and invisible violet. The object of orthochromatic photography is then to transfer the maximum of chemical action, so that it may correspond with this scale of visual luminosity; in other words, to bring the visual and photographic impressions into harmony. An ordinary unorthochromatised plate can be made by proper screening to render correctly all luminosities, but with such a plate the exposures are enormous, and its use, therefore, is not practicable.

Orthochromatic photography is, roughly speaking, to be obtained by using colouring matters to increase and make uniform the sensitiveness of the film to all the visible rays of the spectrum.

Draper's Law of Absorption says that it is only rays which are absorbed that can produce any chemical effect. The rays to which a body may be photo-sensitive can be told from its absorption spectra, except that towards the red end of the spectrum many observers have noticed that there is a very slight shifting as regards the sensitiveness compared with the absorption. "This displacement of the band of absorption (and chemical activity) towards the red is believed to be in accordance with Kundt's law, which asserts that the absorption band of colouring matter is displaced towards the red as the refractive power of the medium in which the substance is dissolved increases." Silver bromide with which dry plates are sensitised mainly absorbs violet or blue rays, and it is therefore light of this colour by which it is chiefly affected, while the yellow rays produce little or no effect.

It is now possible by taking advantage of Dr. Vogel's discovery and by using certain colouring matters – which must be of the complementary colour to that it is desired to absorb – to render the film sensitive to any particular rays, and to obtain photographs much more true to the aspects of nature as regards relative brightness of tints. I say "much more true" advisedly, as coloured objects have two scales of contrasts – contrasts of colour and contrasts of light and shade. It is obvious that **contrasts of Colour cannot be Represented** in black and white. So that it only remains for us to correctly represent light and shade.

Theoretically, no screen should be required for an orthochromatic plate, but such perfection has not yet been obtained. There are now on the market several principal orthochromatic plates, from which amateurs who do not wish to make their own plates may choose. None of these plates give exactly what we require.

The action of the dyes is usually to sensitise only bands of the spectrum, and though several of these bands, due to the use of different dyestuffs, may render a plate sensitive to the whole visible spectrum, its sensitiveness is cut up into different bands with more or less insensitive gaps. The maximum of action is still in the blue and invisible violet, and therefore in order to secure perfect results it is still necessary to use a colour filter in the camera.

The function of the colour filter is threefold. Firstly, it must cut out completely the invisible ultra-violet rays – a factor of which Mr. F. E. Ives has already spoken very emphatically. Secondly, it must reduce the action of the blue; and thirdly, depending upon the colour sensitiveness of the plate, in a lesser degree the green or the red also, unless the plate be equally sensitive to the green and red rays for equal luminosities.

The correct representation of colour according to luminosity has been the dream of all lovers of photography for very many years, but the practical difficulties, in the commercial production of plates and correct light filters, have been enormous, so that it is only quite lately that we amateurs have, through the exertions of Sir William Abney, Mr. Cadett, Mr. Sanger Shepherd, Mr. Saville Kent, and their fellow workers, been able to obtain a plate and screen correctly adjusted to each other. **May we use them wisely and well**.

It is by Sir William Abney's invention of the colour sensitometer that it has been made possible to produce the correct light filters commercially. Every care is taken in producing these filters. A most perfect apparatus was devised by Mr. Cadett and Mr. Sanger Shepherd for measuring the luminosities, and this apparatus was shown and fully described at the Camera Club lately by Mr. James Cadett. The filter is now called by Mr. Cadett the "Absolutus," and consists of four components – two films of coloured gelatine coated on optically worked glass, and two collodion films, the whole being cemented together in optical contact, with Canada balsam. All possible pains is naturally taken to get each film as nearly the correct tint of colour as may be, but with every care the visual test is of very little value. The film is cutting out what the eye does not see. Out of a batch of ten filters which to the eye appear all exactly alike, perhaps four or five will be too far out (Mr. Sanger Shepherd informs me) to pass.

Of this filter Sir William Abney, in his recent lecture at the Royal Photographic Society on screens for three-colour work, says that such a screen is perfect for any kind of light which gives a continuous spectrum. It was with great reluctance that Messrs. Cadett and Neall placed on the market a second light filter which they called the "Gilvus," which from a scientific point of view is not corrected for all colour luminosities with the spectrum plate. It was done in answer to many requests for a screen to be used in such cases where the long exposure with the correct rendering of colour luminosities was not practically feasible. They, however, still recommend the perfect screen to be used whenever possible.

Owing to the difficulties in the production of the spectrum plate, a small portion of the spectrum has to be taken from the sensitiveness of the plate in the extreme red, in order to give a light by which the plates may be manufactured, and manipulated.

It is necessary largely to diminish the blue, and somewhat diminish the green, so as to level up the sensitiveness for equal luminosities of blue, green, and red, in order to obtain absolute correction. This, of course, necessitates increased exposure, and until it is possible so to increase the red sensitiveness of the plate as to enable the light yellow screen to be used for a correct rendering of the luminosity of the red and green rays, only a less correct representation can be obtained.

Before passing on to the reproductions made from some of my experiments in the use of the spectrum plates, I will ask the reader carefully to study the diagrams of the coloured star which I have had made from the one sent out by Mr. Cadett with his pamphlet on orthochromatic photography.

[...]

We see by these examples that the use of the spectrum plate is indicated when there is any great contrast of colour, so that by proper screening, correctly to render all the luminosities; but even where the screening is not practicable, from the length of exposure which would then be necessary, the spectrum plate gives greatly improved results in interiors, with dark oak seats and woodwork, or where the painted glass windows act as a screen; and it produces less violent contrasts than an ordinary plate would do if used.

[...]

The copying in monochrome of coloured pictures has always been a difficulty, but I think that now with a spectrum plate, and orange light filter, an amateur will find the difficulties greatly diminished. When paintings are modern and bright, good results can be obtained by placing them in evenly diffused light, but old dark pictures require an intense light. Mr Ives is said to copy them in direct sunlight; in a very bright light you get detail in deep shadows which at other times is never seen.

[. . .]

There seems to me to be an advantage in using the spectrum plates in the evening when the light is becoming yellow. The picture of the "After-glow" (page 557) was taken a long time after the sun had actually set and the sky was red and gold from the afterglow. The "Absolutus" filter was used, and one minute's exposure given.

"Broad Street at Night" was photographed on a very rapid plate with four hours' exposure. The lens was stopped down to f/11 for one hour, and then the iris diaphragm was carefully turned to the full aperture f/5. The exposure was from eight p.m. to midnight. The hanging lamps were a deep red.

From: Sarah Angelina Acland, "The Spectrum Plate. Theory: Practice: Result," *Photography*, vol. 12, no. 615 (August 23, 1900), 553–560.

24

In Camera

Yevonde

Photographers have little or no sense of colour and if they ever possessed such a quality it has become warped or non-existent through years of disuse. Photographers, in fact, have become so engrossed in the beauty of light and shade and in their deep velvety blacks and sparkling whites that they will tell you quite seriously that the colour photograph is unnecessary and unnatural.

I was to find the general public as biased against the colour photograph as the photographers themselves. Not only did they refuse to pay to have themselves photographed in colour but they would not even look at the specimens I showed them.

To understand this point of view it is necessary to visualise a world entirely without colour, that is to say, a photographic world.

You must imagine yourself with a grey face and a black mouth kissing a girl of similar colouring. If you were a generous sort of person (or very much in love or anxious to create an impression) you would go to a florists and buy her a bouquet of black, white or grey flowers; then you would sit in her black, white or grey room and talk to her mother with a white or grey face and black mouth, dressed in black, white or grey.

If your future mother-in-law looked with favour on your suit she might ask you to stay to lunch. She would feed you on black roast beef, and if the potatoes were white the cabbage would certainly be black or grey, you would drink black beer and the peaches would be grey and the oranges black. (If viewed as a photograph taken on a pan-plate, the oranges would appear light grey, which photographers consider to be "much nearer an orange colour than black".)

After lunch you would stroll in the gardens and gaze on black geraniums, and sit on a white lawn under black trees. At a dance your partners would have grey faces and black mouths and the champagne would be grey, the caviar and the clothes of the men alone retaining their natural colour. The next morning you would wake up to a breakfast of black bacon and black-and-white eggs. What a strange world! And yet, if you had never known a different one, how peculiar the normal coloured world would appear! You would stare in amazement at a girl with red hair and turn in disgust from good red beef. A blue sky would appear crude, and eggs and bacon in their true colours quite uneatable. Yet this, in fact, is what has happened in photography: people have become so used to photographs in black and white that a colour photograph seems to them to be an error in taste.

This curious outlook may be attributed partly also to the poor quality of early experiments both in films and still photographs, and also to the painted photograph, which is something entirely different.

I always felt that the criticism about colour photography being unnatural was bunk, and that even though the process was still in its infancy it opened up a new world to the photographer. Red hair, uniforms, exquisite complexions and coloured finger-nails came into their own. Hurrah! We were in for exciting times!

It was difficult to decide how to set about making beautiful colour photographs because the colour photograph, an entirely new medium, must be more nearly related to the portrait painted by an imaginative artist than to its blood relation the passport photograph.

Realising this, I decided to take colour photographs in a large size, 15 ins. by 12 ins. The colour photograph was to be something precious, not to be doled out in dozens like cabinets or *cartes de visites*.

From: Yevonde, *In Camera* (London: The Woman's Book Club, 1940), Chapter XV1, 184–187.

BIBLIOGRAPHY

Publications to 1900

A Popular Treatise on the Art of Photography. Glasgow: Richard Griffin and Co., 1841.

Acland, Sarah Angelina. "The Spectrum Plate. Theory: Practice: Result," *Photography*, 12, no. 615 (August 23, 1900): 553–560.

An Essay on Combustion. Philadelphia: James Humphreys, 1810.

"Art Treasures Exhibition." *The Literary Gazette*, no. 2106 (May 30, 1857): 519–521.

Atkins, A. A. (Anna). *Photographs of British Algae: Cyanotype Impressions*. 3 vols. Halstead Place, Sevenoaks: privately published, 1843–1853.

Beard, Richard. *Further Improvements in Photography*. London: Steamhouse Press, 1843.

Bingham, Robert J. *Photogenic Manipulation*. London: George Knight & Sons, 1850.

Brewster, David. "Photogenic Drawing, or Drawing by the Agency of Light," *Edinburgh Review*, 76 (1843): 309–344.

"Busy with the Photograph," *Household Words*, 9, no. 214 (April 29, 1854): 242–245.

Clark, Georgina C. "A New and Easy Process of Painting in Oil Colours," *Lady's Own Paper*, October 1868, 258.

Cole, William. "A Letter from Mr. William Cole, member of Bristol, to the Philosophical Society of Oxford: containing his observations on the purple fish," *Philosophical Transactions of the Royal Society*, 15 (1685): 1278–1286.

Cole, William. *PURPURA ANGLICANA, being a discovery of a shell-fish found on the shores of the Severn, in which there is a vein containing a juice giving the delicate and durable tincture of the ancient, rich, Tyrian purple . . .* London: Joseph Streater, 1689.

"Colouring Photographs." No. I, *The Lady's Newspaper & Pictorial Times*, London, January 31, 1863, Issue 840, 244–245.

"Colouring Photographs." No. II, *The Lady's Newspaper & Pictorial Times*, London, February 7, 1863, Issue 841, 253.

"Colouring Photographs." No. III, *The Lady's Newspaper & Pictorial Times*, London, February 21, 1863, Issue 843, 300.

"Colouring Photographs." No. IV, *The Lady's Newspaper & Pictorial Times*, London, March 7, 1843, Issue 845, 341.

Davy, Sir Humphry. *The Collected Works of Sir Humphry Davy, ed. by his brother John Davy, vol. II Early Miscellaneous Papers*. London: Smith, Elder & Co., 1839.

Eastlake, Charles. trans. *Theory of Colours*, Johann Wolfgang von Goethe. London: John Murray, 1840.

Eastlake, Lady Elizabeth. "Photography," *London Quarterly Review*, 101 (April 1857): 442–468.

"English Woman's Conversazione," *The English Woman's Domestic Magazine*, October 1, 1867, issue 34.

"English Woman's Conversazione," *The English Woman's Domestic Magazine*, June 1869, issue 54, 325.

Fisher, George Thomas. *Photogenic Manipulation: Containing Plain Instructions. Illustrated by Woodcuts*. London: George Knight & Sons, 1843.

"French Discovery – Pencil of Nature, from 'The New Art,'" *The Literary Gazette*, issue 1150 (February 2, 1839): 74.

Fulhame, Elizabeth. *An Essay on Combustion, with a View to a New Art of Dying and Painting*. London: J. Cooper, 1794.

Helmholz, Hermann von. *Physiological Optics*. 1856.

Herschel, Sir John F. W. "Note on the Art of Photography, or the Application of the Chemical Rays of Light to the Purposes of Pictorial Representation," [abstract] *Proceedings of the Royal Society*, 4, no. 37, 1839.

Herschel, John. "On the Chemical Action of the Rays of the Solar Spectrum on Preparations of Silver and other Substances, both metallic and non-metallic, and on some Photographic Processes," *Philosophical Transactions of the Royal Society*, 130 (1840): 1–59.

Herschel, John. "On the Action of the Rays of the Solar Spectrum on Vegetable Colours, and on Some New Photographic Processes," *Philosophical Transactions of the Royal Society of London*, 132 (1842): 181–214.

Herschel, Julia. *A Handbook for Greek and Roman Lace Making*. London: R. Barrett & Sons, 1869.

Hill, L. L. *A Treatise on Heliochromy; or the production of Pictures, by means of Light in Natural Colours*. New York: Robinson & Caswell, 1856.

Hunt, Robert. *A Manual of Photography*, 3rd edition enlarged. London: John Joseph Griffin and Co., 1853.

Hunt, Robert. "On the Application of Science to the Fine and Useful Arts." "Heliochrome," *The Art Journal*, October 1851, 257–258.

Hunt, William Holman. "Address to the London Society of Arts," *Journal of the Society of Arts* (April 23, 1880): 485–499.

Joly, John. "On a Method of Photography in Natural Colours," *The British Journal of Photography*, 42, no. 1857 (December 6, 1895): 774–776.

"Journal of Science, Inventions and Improvements: Mr Beard's Further Improvements to Photography," *The Critic*, London, 3, no. 68 (April 18, 1846): 435.

Laman, Samuel. ed. *George Cruikshank's Omnibus, Illustrated with One Hundred Engravings*, London: Blanchard, 1842.

Le Blon, J. C. *Coloritto or the Harmony of Colouring in Painting: reduced to mechanical practice*. London, 1720.

Le Blon, J. C. *Coloritto or the Harmony of Colouring in Painting*. 1756, facsimile edition with intro. by Faber Birren, New York: Van Nostrand Reinhold Company, 1980.

Lippmann, Gabriel. "Colour Photography," *Nature*, 53, no. 1383 (April 30, 1896): 617–618.

Lock, S. R. "Coloured Photographs," *The Photographic and Fine Art Journal* (April 1855): 111.

Mansion, L. *Letters Upon the Art of Miniature Painting*. London: R. Ackerman, 1822.

Maxwell, James Clerk. "On the Theory of Compound Colours and the Relations of the Colours of the Spectrum," *Philosophical Transactions of the Royal Society of London*, 150 (1860): 57–84.

Maxwell, James Clerk. "On the Theory of Three Primary Colours," *Proceedings of the Royal Institution of Great Britain*, 3, 1858–1862 (May 17, 1861): 370–374.

Morley, Henry and Wills, William. "Photography" *Household Words*, 7, no. 156 (March 19, 1853): 54–61.

Morris, William. *Hopes and Fears for Art*. London: Ellis & White, 1882.

Newman, J. *The Principles and Practice of Harmonious Colouring in Oil, Water and Photographic Colours on Paper, Glass and Silver-Plate, by an Artist Photographer.* London: Cassell, Petter & Galpin, 1859.

Newman, J. *Harmonious Colouring as Applied to Photographs*. London: Newman, 1863.

Newton, Sir Isaac. *Opticks: or a Treatise on the Reflections, Refractions, and Colours of Light.* 3rd ed. London: William & John Innys, 1721.

Niven, W. D. ed. *The Scientific Letters and Papers of James Clerk Maxwell.* Cambridge: Cambridge University Press, 1890.

"Photographic Colouration." *The Athenaeum*, London, no. 1017 (April 24, 1847): 440.

"Photographic Experiments," *Mechanics' Magazine, Museum, Register, Journal and Gazette*, no. 1175 (February 14, 1846): 143–144.

"Photographic Failures," *Punch*, 12, no. 299 (April 3, 1847): 143.

"Photographic Notes," *Journal of the Birmingham Photographic Society*, III, 1850.

"Photographic Portraits," *Cleave's Penny Gazette of Variety and Amusement*, May 14 (1842), issue 31.

"Photography in Natural Colours, &c," *American Journal of Photography and the Allied Arts & Sciences*, 8, no. 15 (February 1, 1866): 342–345.

Pliny the Elder. *The Natural History*, trans. John Bostock and H. T. Riley. London: Taylor & Francis, 1855.

Root, Marcus Aurelius. *The Camera and the Pencil; or the Heliographic Art.* Philadelphia, New York, 1864.

Ruskin, John. *The Complete Works of John Ruskin* (Library Edition), ed. E. T. Cook and Alexander Wedderburn. London: George Allen, 1903–1912, 39 vols.

"Since This Old Cap was New," *All the Year Round*, no. 30 (November 19, 1859): 76–80.

Talbot, William Henry Fox. "Some Account of the Art of Photogenic Drawing, or the Process by Which Natural Objects May be Made to Delineate Themselves Without the Aid of the Artist's Pencil," *Philosophical Magazine*, XIV (1839): 196–208.

Talbot, William Henry Fox. "Some Experiments on Coloured Flames," *The Edinburgh Journal of Science*, 5 no. 1 (July 1826): 77–81.

The Art Union, June 1, 1845, 171.

The Correspondence of William Henry Fox Talbot, foxtalbot.dmu.ac.uk.

The Pencil of Nature. London: Longman, Brown, Green & Longmans, 1844–1846.

"The Carte De Visite," *All the Year Round*, 7, no. 157 (April 26, 1862): 165–168.

"The Photograph," *Punch*, 41 (July 20, 1861): 32.

"Those Who Live in Glass Houses," *All the Year Round*, XII, no. 292 (November 26, 1864): 372–374.

Wall, Alfred. *A Manual of Artistic Colouring as Applied to Photographs. A Practical Guide to Artists and Photographers.* London, Thomas Piper, 1861.

Young, Thomas. "On the Theory of Light and Colours," *Philosophical Transactions of the Royal Society of London*, 92 (1802): 12–48.

Publications after 1900

Armstrong, Carol and De Zegher, Catherine, eds. *Ocean Flowers: Impressions from Nature.*

Baker, J. T. "Tyrian Purple: an Ancient Dye, a Modern Problem," *Endeavour*, 33, no. 118 (1974): 11–17.

Barthes, Roland. *Camera Lucida: Reflections on Photography*, trans. Richard Howard. New York: Hill & Wang, 1981.

Batchen, Geoffrey. *Burning with Desire: The Conception of Photography.* Boston: MIT Press, 1997.

Batchen, Geoffrey. *Emanations: the Art of the Cameraless Photograph.* Munich: Prestel, 2016.

Benjamin, Walter. "A Small History of Photography," *One Way Street and Other Writings*, trans. Edmund Jephcott and Kingsley Shorter. London: Verso, 1985.

Bjelkhagen, Hans I. "Lippmann Photography: Reviving an Early Colour Process," *History of Photography*, 23, no. 3 (Autumn 1999): 274–280.

Burch, R. M. *Colour Printing and Colour Printers*. New York: The Baker & Taylor Co., 1910.

Cat, Jordi. *Maxwell, Sutton, and the Birth of Colour Photography*. Basingstoke: Palgrave, 2013.

Coe, Brian. *Colour Photography: the First Hundred Years 1840–1940*. London: Ash & Grant, 1978.

Cotton, Charlotte. "Nine Years, a Million Conceptual Miles," www.aperture.org/magazine-2013

Daly, Nicholas. *Sensation and Modernity in the 1860s*. Cambridge: Cambridge University Press, 2009.

Davenport, Derek A. and Ireland, Kathleen M. "The Ingenious, Lively and Celebrated Mrs Fulhame and the Dyer's Hand," *Bulletin History of Chemistry*, 5 (1989): 37–42.

Dullaway, Sanna. www.sannadullaway.com/about

Edwards, Steve. *The Making of English Photography: Allegories*. Pennsylvania: Penn State University Press, 2006.

Gage, John. *Colour and Culture, Practice and Memory: Practice and Meaning from Antiquity to Abstraction*. London: Thames & Hudson, 2000.

Gaskill, Nicholas. *Chromographia: American Literature and the Modernization of Color*. Minneapolis: University of Minnesota Press, 2018.

Grasselli, Margaret Morgan. *Colourful Impressions: the Print Making Revolution in Eighteenth-Century France*. Washington, DC. National Gallery of Art, 2003.

Green-Lewis, Jennifer. *Victorian Photography, Literature and the Invention of Modern Memory*. London: Bloomsbury, 2017.

Hannavy, John. *Victorian Photographers at Work*. Princes Risborough: Shire, 1997.

Henderson, Giles. *Sarah Angelina Acland: First Lady of Colour Photography, 1849–1930*. Oxford: Bodleian Library, 2012.

Henisch, Heinz K. and Bridget A., *The Painted Photograph 1839–1914, Origins, Techniques, Aspirations*. Pennsylvania: Penn State University Press, 1996.

Hirsch, Robert. *Exploring Colour Photography: a Complete Guide*. 5th ed. New York: Focal Press, 2001.

Hyper, Philip. "Colours in Photography, the Problem Resolved," *History of Photography*, 23, no. 3 (Autumn 1999): 281–293.

Isler-de-Jongh, Ariane. "The Origins of Colour Photography," *History of Photography*, 18, no. 2 (Summer 1994): 111–119.

Jacob, Michael. "Colour and the Daguerreotype," *Daguerreotype Journal* (June 2014): 12–19.

Jammes, André and Janis, Eugenia. *The Art of the French Calotype*. Princeton: Princeton University Press, 1983.

Jeffrey, Ian. *Revisions; an Alternative History of Photography*. Bradford: National Museum of Photography, Film and Television, 1999.

Kalba, Laura Anne. *Color in the Age of Impressionism: Commerce, Technology, and Art*. University Park: Penn State University Press, 2017.

Keller, Dana. "My Photo-Shop Story, Dana Keller Colorizer," www.petapixel.com/201

Kingsley, Hope. "Round Table Two," *Salt & Silver, Early Photography 1840–1860, from the Wilson Collection*. London: Tate, 2015.

Loske, Alexandra. *Color: A Visual History from Newton to Modern Color Matching Guides*. Washington, DC: Smithsonian Books, 2019.

Mavor, Carol. *Blue Mythologies: Reflections on a Colour*. London: Reaktion Books, 2013.

Maynard, Patrick. "Talbot's Technologies: Photographic Depiction, Detection, and Reproduction," *Journal of Aesthetics and Art Criticism*, 47, no. 3 (Summer 1989): 263–276.

O'Hagan, Sean. "The Music's Here Then It's Gone Like a Dream," *Observer*, November 19, 2017, 6–8.

Packer, Lelia and Sliwka, Jennifer. *Monochrome: Painting in Black and White*. London: National Gallery, 2017.

Pritchard, Michael, ed., *Technology and Art: the Birth and Early Years of Photography*. Bath: Royal Photographic Society, 1990.

Ribeyrol, Charlotte, ed. *The Colours of the Past in Victorian England*. Bern: Peter Lang, 2016.

Rinhart, F. and Rinhart, M. *The American Daguerreotype*. Athens: Georgia University Press, 1981.

Ryan, James. "Placing Early Photography: the Work of Robert Hunt in Mid-Nineteenth Century Britain," *History of Photography*, 41, no. 4 (2017): 343–361.

Schaaf, Larry. *Out of the Shadows: Herschel, Talbot & the Invention of Photography*. New Haven: Yale University Press, 1992.

Schaaf, Larry. *Records of the Dawn of Photography: Talbot's Notebooks P and Q*. Cambridge: Cambridge University Press, 1996.

Schaaf, Larry. "Sir John Herschel's 1839 Royal Society Paper on Photography," *History of Photography*, 3, no. 1 (1979): 47–60.

Schaaf, Larry. *Sun Gardens: Cyanotypes by Anna Atkins*. Munich: Prestel, 2018.

Schaaf, Larry. "The First Fifty Years of British Photography: 1794–1844," in Michael Pritchard, ed., *Technology and Art: the Birth and Early Years of Photography*, 9–18. Bath: Royal Photographic Society, 1990.

Schwarz, Heinrich. *Art and Photography: Forerunners and Influences*. Chicago: University of Chicago Press, 1985.

Sherman, Paul D. *Colour Vision in the Nineteenth Century: the Young/Helmholz/Maxwell Theory*. Bristol: Adam Hilger, 1981.

Siapkas, Johannes and Sjögren, Lena. *Displaying the Ideals of Antiquity*. New York: Routledge, 2014.

Siegal, Steffen. *First Exposures: Writings from the Beginnings of Photography*. Los Angeles: Getty Publications, 2017.

Smith, Lindsay. *Victorian Photography, Painting and Poetry*. Cambridge: Cambridge University Press, 1995.

Smith, Lindsay. *The Politics of Focus: Women, Children and Nineteenth Century Photography*. Manchester: Manchester University Press, 1998.

Smith, Lindsay. "Thinking Blues," *Transactions and Encounters: Science and Culture in the Nineteenth Century*, ed. Roger Luckhurst and Josephine McDonagh, 55–74. Manchester: Manchester University Press, 2002.

Snyder, Joel. "*Res Ipsa Loquitur*," in Lorraine Daston, ed., *Things that Talk, Object Lessons from Art and Science*, 195–220. New York: Zone Books, 2004.

Taylor, Roger and Ware, Mike. "Pilgrims of the Sun: the Chemical Evolution of the Calotype 1840–1852," *History of Photography*, 27, no. 4 (2003): 308–319.

Timby, Kim. "Colour Photography and Stereoscopy: Parallel Histories," *History of Photography*, 29, no. 2 (Summer 2005): 183–196.

Ware, Mike. *Cyanotype: The History, Science, and Art of Photographic Printing in Prussian Blue*. London: Science Museum and National Museum of Photography, Film and Television, 1999.

Ware, Mike. "Herschel's Chrysotype: A Golden Legend Re-told," *History of Photography*, 30, no. 1 (Spring 2006): 1–24.

Watson, Roger and Rappaport, Helen. *Capturing the Light*. London: Macmillan, 2013.

Wild, Wolfgang and Lloyd, Jordan. *History as They Saw It: Iconic Moments from the Past in Color*. San Francisco: Chronicle Books, 2018.

Wittgenstein, Ludwig. *Remarks on Colour*, ed. G. E. M. Anscombe, trans. Linda McAlister and Margaret Schattle. Berkeley: University of California Press, 1978.

Yevonde, *In Camera*. London: The Woman's Book Club, 1940.

INDEX

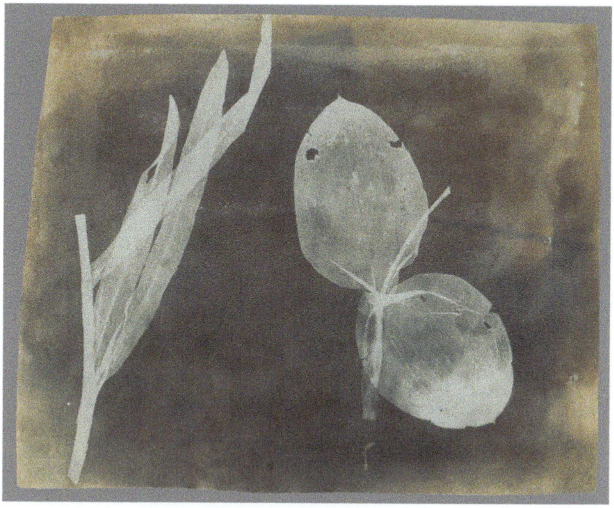

PLATE 1 William Henry Fox Talbot, *Leaves of Orchidea* (April 1839), photogenic drawing, salted paper print.

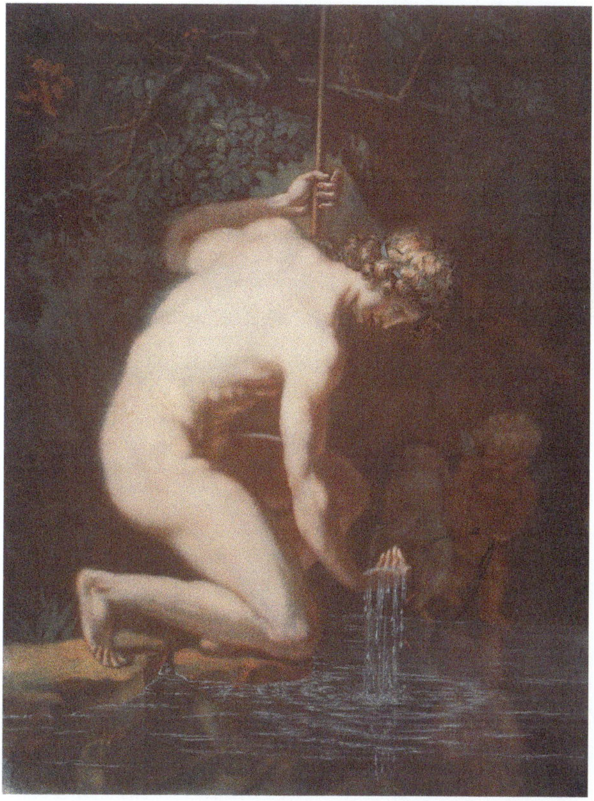

PLATE 2 J. C. Le Blon, *Narcissus* (1714), colour mezzotint.

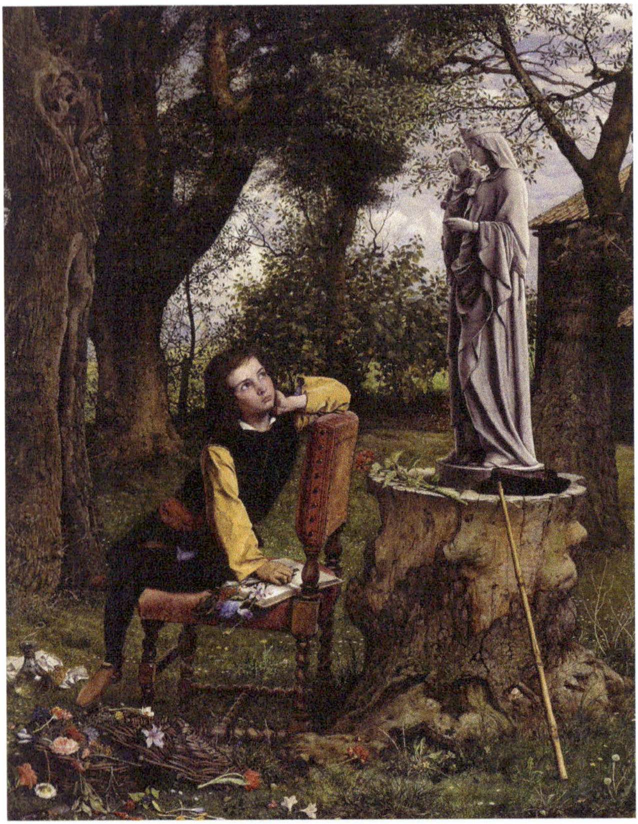

PLATE 3 William Dyce, *Titian Preparing to Make First Lesson in Colouring* (1856–1857), oil on canv

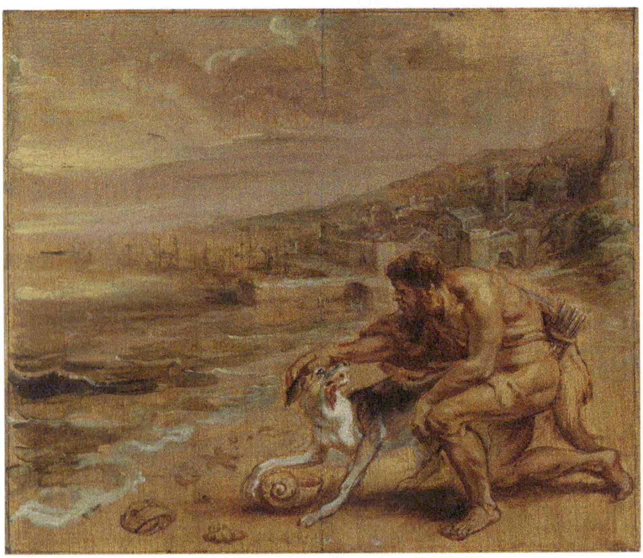

PLATE 4 Peter Paul Rubens, *Heracles's Dog discovers the Purple Dye* (1636), oil on canvas.

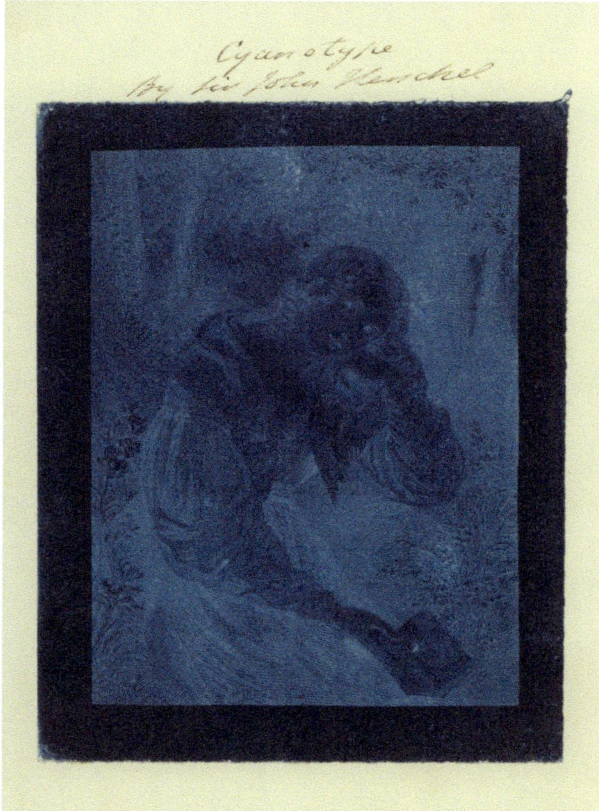

PLATE 5 Sir John Herschel, *Engraved Portrait of a Young Woman* (about 1842), cyanotype.

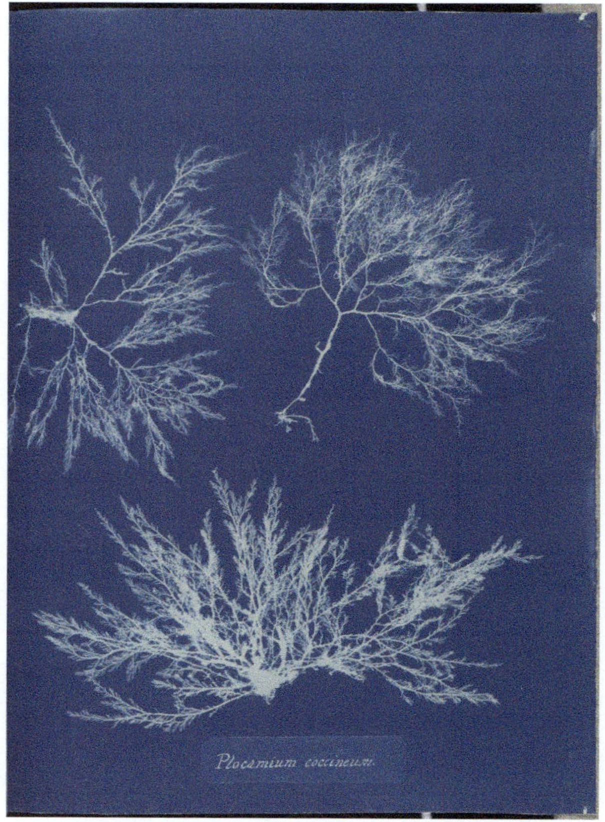

PLATE 6 Anna Atkins, *Plocamium coccineum* (1846–1847), cyanotype.

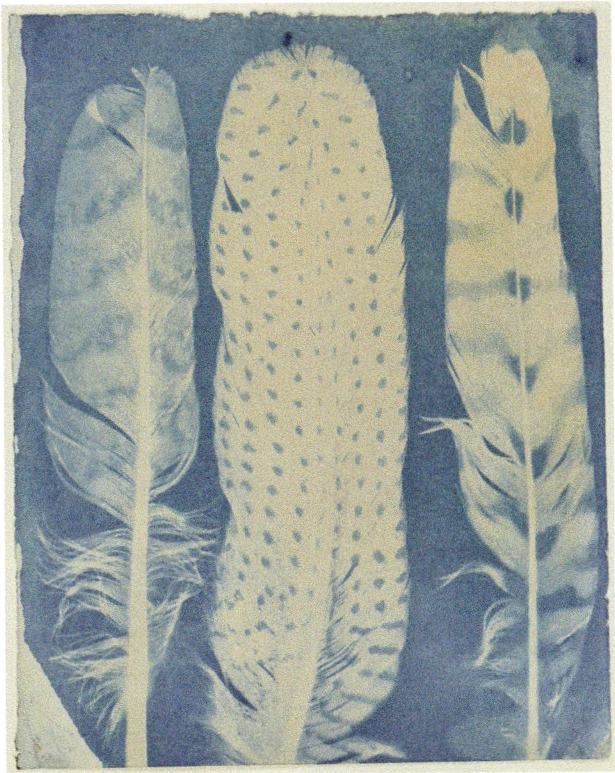

PLATE 7 Hippolyte Bayard, *Three feathers* (1840–1841), cyanotype.

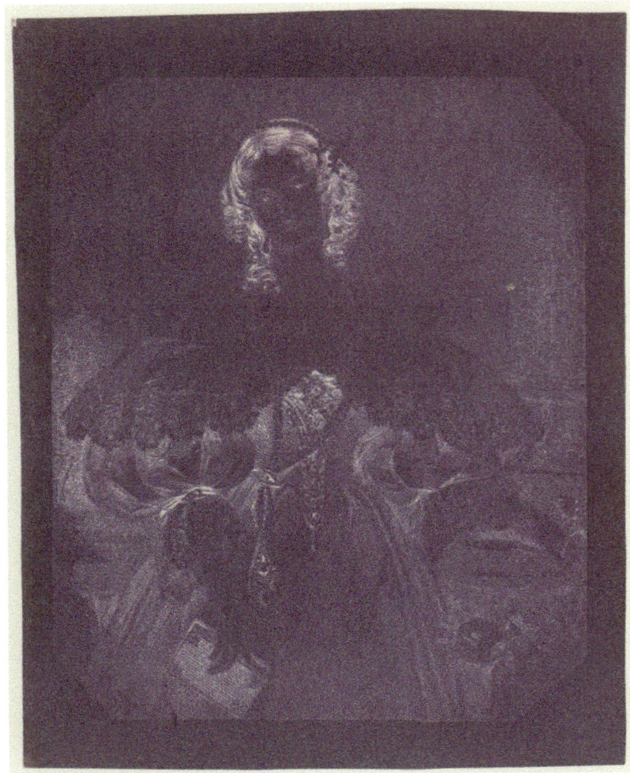

PLATE 8 Sir John Herschel, *Experimental photogenic drawing* (1842), chrysotype.

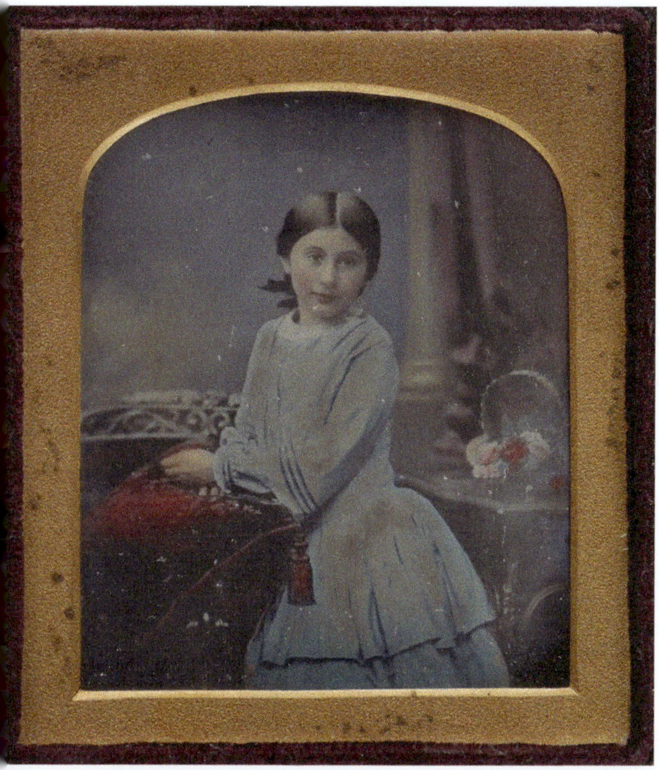

PLATE 9 Antoine-François-Jean Claudet (1797–1867), *Portrait of a Girl in a Blue Dress* (about 1854), daguerreotype, hand-tinted.

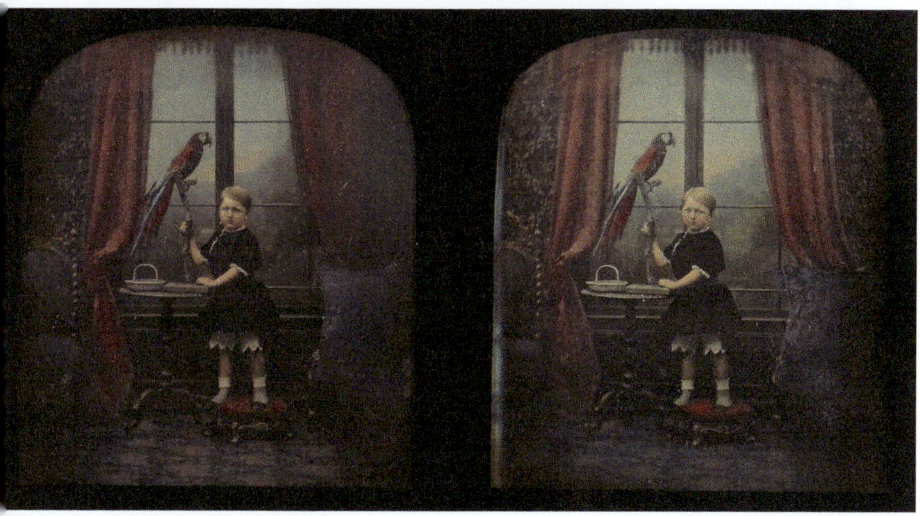

LATE 10 Antoine-François-Jean Claudet (1797–1867), *Boy with a Parrot* (about 356), hand-colored stereographic daguerreotype.

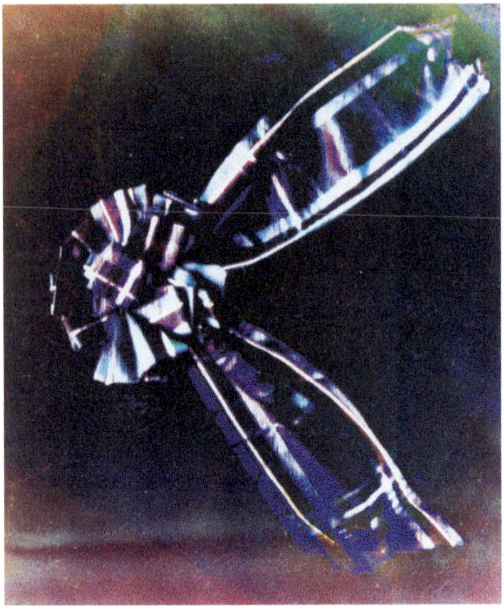

PLATE 11 Thomas Sutton/James Clerk Maxwell, *Tartan Ribbon* (1861), tri-color negatives.

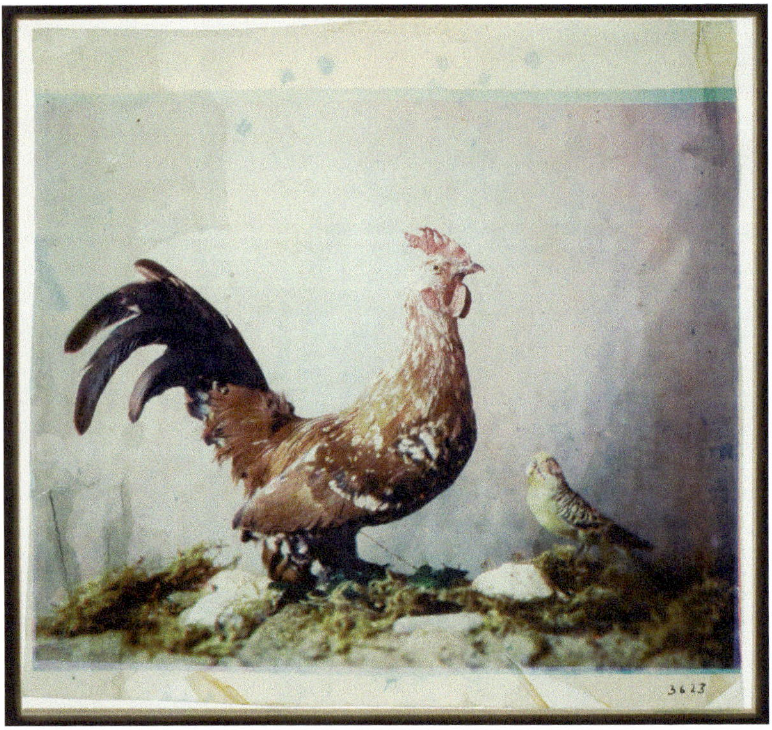

PLATE 12 Louis Ducos du Hauron, *Still Life with Rooster* (c. 1869–1879), transparency, three-color carbon.

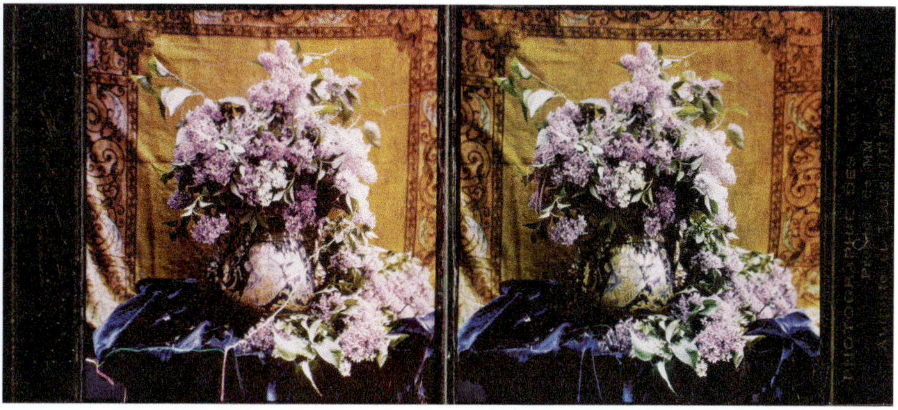

PLATE 13 Lumière Brothers *Lilacs* (about 1898), autochrome, stereograph.

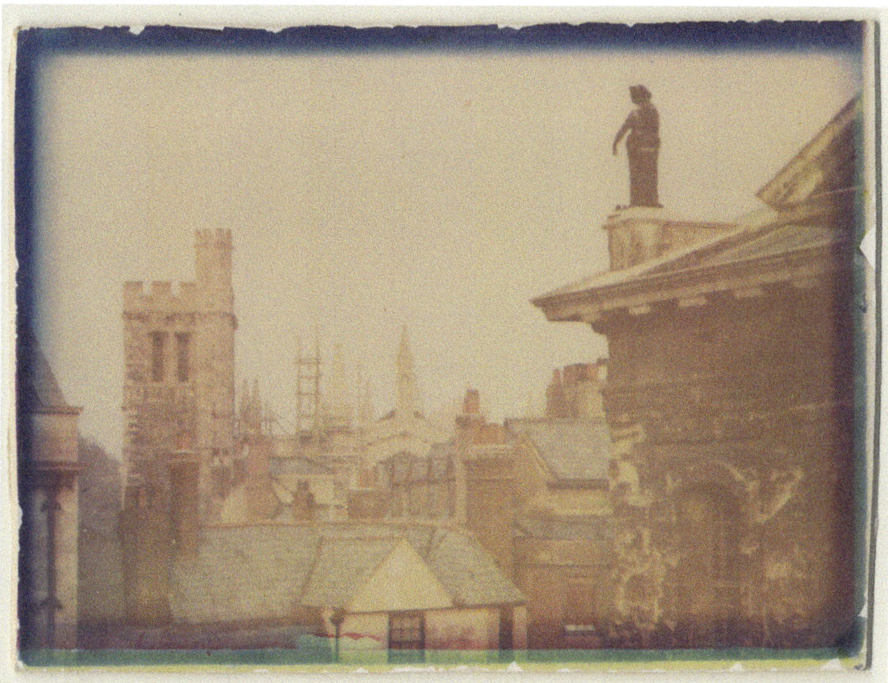

PLATE 14 Sarah Angelina Acland, *Broad Street, Oxford* (around 1900), color print from three-color separation glass negatives.

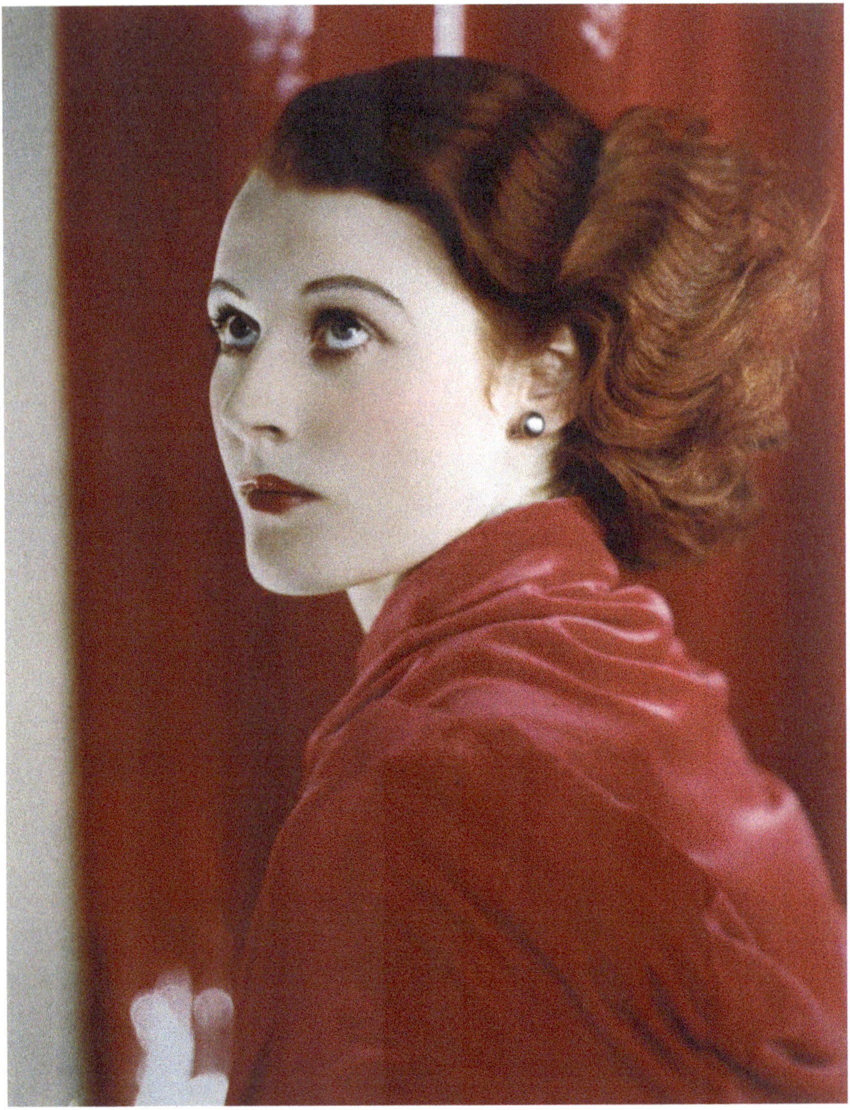

PLATE 15 Yevonde, *Joan Maude* (1932), Vivex colour print.